John Minczeski

THE RECONSTRUCTION OF LIGHT

Minnesota Voices Project #2

John Minczeski

The Reconstruction of Light

Drawings by Alvaro Cardona-Hine

New Rivers Press 1981

Copyright © 1981 by John Minczeski
Library of Congress Catalog Card Number: 81-80546
ISBN: 0-89823-023-3
All Rights Reserved
Book Design: C. W. Truesdale
Typesetting: Peregrine Cold Type

Some of these poems have appeared in the following publications: *Kansas Quarterly*, *Lake Street Review*, and *Milkweed Chronicle*. Our thanks to the editors of these publications for permission to reprint here.

"Sgt. Pepper Summer: A Memoir" was featured on Garrison Keillor's *Prairie Home Companion* (National Public Radio).

The author wishes to thank the Minnesota State Arts Board for a Works-In-Progress grant which allowed him time to write some of these poems.

New Rivers Press books are distributed by
        Small Press Distribution, Inc.
        Jeanetta Jones Miller
        1784 Shattuck Ave.
        Berkeley, CA 94709

Books published in the Minnesota Voices Project are also distributed regionally by
        Bookslinger
        2163 Ford Parkway
        St. Paul, MN 55116

The Reconstruction of Light has been manufactured in the United States of America for New Rivers Press, Inc. (C. W. Truesdale, editor/publisher), 1602 Selby Ave., St. Paul, MN 55104 in a first edition of 1,000 copies of which 20 have been signed and numbered by John Minczeski and Alvaro Cardona-Hine.

For Joan

The Reconstruction of Light

I.

11. Solstice
12. Siciliano
13. Nocturne
14. Lucha
15. Sunrise/Spoleto 1967

II.

19. The Fight Against Gravity
21. The Flint Hills
22. Oklahoma City
23. Okie Grease Monkey
25. The Green Man (Prelude & Fugue)
29. Sgt. Pepper Summer: A Memoir
36. Enlightenment Comes Yesterday

III.

39. The Shot Gun Of Desire
40. Palm Sunday
41. The Photographs
42. Lost White Brother In Rome
43. The Invention Of Weather
44. The Language Of Animals
46. Nice Serpent
47. Snake Man In Winter
49. To Measure The Hand
50. The Moon's Scars
52. Snake To His Lost Love
54. Five Nocturnes

IV.

61. Lot's Wife In The Twentieth Century
64. Wild Rose
65. Name Of The Muse
68. Old Ego Song
69. Vivaldi Lives
70. Poland: Current Events
71. The Invention Of Silence
72. Tzara
75. The Reconstruction Of Light
77. The Detective

I

Solstice

When you look into your eyes
in hotels, bars, the Mississippi,
you call your name over and over—
John, is that you?

On the farm a bob cat once sat by the birches
watching the farm house for hours, running
away whenever you approached. It was winter.

One evening you drove past the old stump
at the bend in the drive & it sat there
licking its paw. When you stopped the car
and turned to look, it was gone.

Your father, your grandfather, they
knew how to keep things where they belonged;
the wheelbarrow turned upside down by the garage,
the fork and rake against the wall.

*

It is wearing into December,
and Handel is on the record player—
"Comfort ye, my people."

The light wears out early
I grow tired early
telling myself it is only this season.

If only it were Christmas already
looking up from the bottom of the well
with money in my pocket for a change.

At 4 o'clock the snowstorm and the sun
begin wearing out at the same time.
Our wakes have disappeared into the early night.

No matter. Looking back from the future
we won't know who lived here
or what became of them.

Siciliano

Evening floats by. It is the tugboat of night
pulling night around and around the earth.
For the earth is its river, it says. The young
fill their cups, the old slowly pour theirs back.

Three grey squirrels chase around a grey elm.
Buildings disappear in the grey night.
The ferry boat shoves off
a single bird is chirping.

How odd the old alchemist is still awake
and a clarinet goes on all evening.

The dreams buried in the garden
slowly drag themselves out again
and call to the wind.
The day yawns. We are swallowed
into the grave of honeysuckle, of summer.

Nocturne

Birds are singing beyond the window,
it is always winter when the fire burns low.
The fisherman plods up the hill with a single fish.
Where does the wind blow nights like this?

Night forms in the embers of the day
the wick that always burns thin.
There is no injury that cannot adapt
to the broken threads that remain our home.

The doctor whispers to himself as he blows out his lamp
What sweetness we take from each other we give
to ourselves. The shape of the recluse fixes itself
on the dawn my love, as if from heaven it falls.

Delmore Schwartz is dead, and Weldon Kees.
The dark light is also beautiful, the branches
curl against the tree. The wind blows tenderly
as if from heaven it falls, my love, as if from heaven it falls.

Lucha

for Michael Delaney

Midnight. Thinking you are with a lover
I do not call, as I have not called
for the last fourteen years. The phone
hangs limp on its cradle.
A small worker in a world of workers.

A magazine ad showing a ship laying cable.
A diagram from the fifties showing
how Russian trawlers cut the cable
stopping conversations between capitalists.
Now the Russians are in Kabul
where you were drummed out of the peace corps.

I wrote you on the day you were "de-selected",
said it was better to learn Persian than teach
English. Now I wonder if the future
will catch up to us. If he'll carry his own
welcome mat as he stands at the door
& assures us there'll always be sparrows.

I could call the coast
if I was sure there was a coast to call.
We could tell each other
we helped stop a war
as we linked arms with people
in the streets.

Or you could call and say it doesn't matter,
that nothing matters. Sirens in the night
don't matter, night is just another dream
of the sun.

So I just let the phone ring.
In the silence that echoes
from one end of the line to the other
there is a single political truth:
the enemy *is* silence,
we are known by the enemies we keep.

Sunrise/Spoleto 1967

I have looked at my hands for signs
like the scribbled nonsense carpenters leave
inside walls: *Every house knows me but not my father.*

The times you were afraid your arms
would turn into pigeons, we held hands
deep in the night at Angel of Mercy hospital.

Your lips were white, and outside a man trudged
up the hill with a bundle of wood
toward the sun rise.
You smiled faintly and said *the mirror is bloodless.*
I poured myself the last
of the strong coffee in the thermos. The night sounds
of the ward clamoured against the dim bulb on the ceiling.
I went to the door and could not tell which groan was yours.

II

The Fight Against Gravity

My brother showed me how to make dum-dum bullets with an awl so that even a rim-fire cartridge would do more than it was supposed to. He would go with his shotgun buddies down along the river when summer was boiling away the brains of ground hogs and shoot everything that moved. I went to the basement and made dum-dum bullets, thinking of the hole going out on the other side, not knowing the soul needs a large hole. When I went to the farm with my grandfather's .22, a gun his father owned before him, that he shot the dog "rusty" with when it attacked the grandchildren, I blew the head off a yellow-breasted robin. I did what any western man would have done — took careful aim. I squeezed the trigger a few times before cocking it so that the bird's soul would become frozen in the trajectory. It was a steamy afternoon in Indiana. Somewhere north, on the tollroad, crews were erecting three white crosses for the Pennsylvania family whose station wagon went head-on into a bridge abutment. The dum-dum met the neck of the bird and expanded, kept expanding. The silence grew like the inquisition. I looked around to see if my grandmother heard the shot, and dug some earth up behind the barn with the heel of my loafer, as if I were digging a football tee, only a little deeper. Too shallow anyway for a bird, even one without a head. The head was blown clean to heaven. The stump on the body didn't bleed, no feathers flew, another fight against gravity was lost. An hour later, on my way back from the woods, the grave was empty. I began to believe in miracles again and went looking for some music. The thirst for it became insatiable. Two days later I was walking through a record store with a new girlfriend who pointed out Gershwin's *Rhapsody in Blue*. "This is beautiful," she said. I bought the record on the spot. I couldn't kill any more birds either. Not because I didn't try — I wounded a sparrow in a corn-field but my cousin had to finish it off because I missed — even at point-blank range. By now I was scratching crosses on the heads of my bullets. I was closing my eyes more. For Christmas my father gave me a Remington .22. I used it twice. I never told him how the rifle was only an excuse for getting out of the house and being alone in the woods. I told myself too much success leads to failure. Finally, it wouldn't fire, safety on or off. No one understood my sudden transition to pacificism, the hours alone in my room, the turning, the silent bird head perched on top of my own.

The Flint Hills

I remember driving through the flint hills. They were like an ocean with nowhere to go. Giant waves of rock and earth —no trees, no sails, no plume of smoke on the horizon. The hawks soared three feet off the ground, almost motionless in the overcast. They looked like they were sleeping, their heads hung so low, or like old men searching for something in the newspaper, their lips moving as they read. Occasionally one would rise with something dark and sweet caught in its beak, wings slowly flapping. Perhaps another mouse about to become a hawk.

I felt like dancing — pounding the earth, to awaken the skeletons beneath, the jawbones of horses and hawks.

How easy to think they were looking for me —the lost white brother on the lost white highway of Kansas— or looking for something ahead of me: something, don't ask me what, that also dances.

In the afternoon, in Oklahoma, the hawks sat on fenceposts or telephone wires along the roads waiting for a car to run over a skunk, or a mouse, or a cat, or a toad. They didn't care, they have wings.

Oklahoma City

Red clay everywhere especially on the sides of cars fooling me for a moment that this was Gary where the iron oxides and sulphur pour out of pipes that stand crazily in the air and speak to each other with their strange smoke. They are beyond both love and forgiveness, for all that matters to them is that abstract language —volumes and volumes— that filters onto roofs, roads and the human heart. I asked people the meaning of red clay and they turned useless eyes toward me. Were there compass irregularities, difficulties in navigation?
I offered my own hypothesis:

The sun set once on this spot.
It was before Adam and Eve. The earth was in love with the sun.
When they slept together, the heat of the sun
turned the earth red, like a sunset. The red earth became
powdery and settled on the fine clockwork of the sun.
There is a price to all things — even love.
And the sun had to set in the sea
to cool it. The earth remained red because it can never forget.
The ocean is soothing in its way, but we all long for what is hot,
so it goes with the sun now.

We were in a Chinese restaurant eating duck. The others were nodding their heads excitedly. I knew I was onto something. Doesn't the earth glow, only a little, before sunset? And I didn't let on about Gary, Indiana and those tall pipes that contain mysteries too deep for any human to comprehend.

Okie Grease Monkey

for Jack Ledbetter

The words come out under a '57 Rambler,
bolts dropping around the creeper,
telling us to stand back.
If the trannie gets away from you
you'll heave it right where we're standing.

Transmissions, pawls, planetary gears,
bad metal, and your hands, healers.
A dry wind from the refinery tells our faces
the latest news.

And your leathery self-knowledge
Just an Okie grease monkey
that rose in the same breath with
*If a job's worth doing
it's worth doing right*,
quoting my dad, or your dad,
his funny eye drifting
over the blown autumn of Oklahoma.

Last time we counted traffic in Ponca City
we went down for beer at the Pizza Inn.
I'd never argue again with Neal or read
Blake during break hoping for a thunderstorm
so we could knock off early.
You looked at the couples drinking 3.2
and said, "I envy you, Minczeski.
Ain't got nothing but a wife
& them books & you're happy."

I wanted to tell you not to waste your time
feeling bad for yourself. Every Tuesday is a joke
anyway. And each day disappears under our skin.
Maybe they come back sometime, Jack, I don't know.

Maybe you didn't go to Vietnam after Mechanics School
and lie in a field with your leg twisted beneath you
and one day in Houston you forget all about hydraulics
as you watch a woman samba against the grain of traffic.
Your mustache grows and you let your '56 Chevy go to rust.
You stand in line holding a ticket for Brazil.
Do it right, Jack. Say this country has gotten away from you
and you're going to heave it right where we're standing.

The Green Man (Prelude & Fugue)

for David Horne (1948-1978)

One more letter lies salted and abandoned
in the drawer where it waits like great
chunks of ice piled on roofs in January
or signatures read in the mirror
            by monks of darkness.

Rice paper boats sail into lagoons
shaped like chest cavities.
A man kneeling at waters' edge stands
and walks with his back to us through
            blossoming sand plum.

*

You always loved the winter.
Days you would slide down the hill by our apartment
on a broken cardboard box, the snow wet
as ashes falling in Vietnam. It is winter now.
I remain awake — the wind blows stiffly
all night. The back door is almost yanked off its hinges.
The small Texas towns remain that were iced-in last year.
The newspaper is yellowing. It says "The wife of the house
survives."

There were times last year I didn't want to talk.
I wanted to sit by myself
in a large room and gnaw
my knuckles while thinking of the future.
Now it is winter
the leaves are stuck inside the twigs
and there is no future.

I want to bite the dust of April
when the wind has its own chimes.
I want to take the sun
in my mouth like a hot wafer
and clumsily stitch the head

of a scare-crow disguised
in wrap-around sunglasses
holding the steering wheel
of a black Packard in one hand.

I have made a post-card of the scene:
There is a green fire snapping
through corn.
The scarecrow is to the left looking away
from the windbreak. Clear across the field
in a little house, Antonin Dvorak
glances up as he pauses in a string quartet.
Way off in the distance crows appear
as little dots against the severe and blue sky.

There is a foundry in men that works with the molten metal
of women. It is too late
to tell you this now, but I am the green man
the spring pig who has run away. Farmers' wives
and the town carpenter ran after me. I fled
to the deep woods. I could almost feel their hands
& the spit being shoved through my rectum.
In a previous lifetime I failed the part of Hansel.
I could not spell "Character" properly.
Stay with your father, they told me. I built fences
and put in a road to the cottage.
Barn cats went wild at milking time.
When I arrived in America, I kissed the soil.
Nobody wants to be like Robinson Crusoe
and live by routine, become eccentric
in a houseful of cats and spent milk cartons.

We want to live by our wits. Sell off the empire state
building to a desert prince. But there are so few answers.
It's just as well — they'd get gunned down
by some young question wanting to make a name for itself—
Iran, Afghanistan, or your Chevrolet going out of control.

I didn't want clocks to stop a few seconds
before midnight in some cream-colored room

in Clear Lake, Texas where the wife of the house
waits in her house coat all day looking across
the wheat field.

It would be easier if she didn't think
you keep piling into a bridge railing
on the ice of '78 on your way back from the lumber
yard. The Christmas tree in the trunk
twisted in the flame — and geese passed over
on their way north where I saw them a month later
on the road to Fargo. I'll have forgotten how much
like children they are, loud voiced
all giving directions at once.

The Egyptians thought the soul was like a bird
little song bird with a man's head—the *Ka-Bird*.
I didn't want you to have such a bird's-eye
view of the Arkansas River
as your headlights scattered over the ice.

I do not play *Ich Steh mit einem Fus im Grabe*
on my Flauto Dolce though it is night again
and the moon, with a lopsided face, flies above the shadows
of the back yard, the snow almost blue.

Tell me the night doesn't sleep. Tell me there were nights
you listened to your heart beating as you heard
the traffic unroll through the window on MacKubin Street.
And when you spread out your bedding in the front room, you
saw the picture of Anubis on the bookcase.
I didn't know you carried the book of the dead with you.
There are still days I cannot break the seams of my silence
but I always thought fire could be our friend
even now as I light a cigarette, as I've so often done, and say
Let the fire be good, let the fire be good.

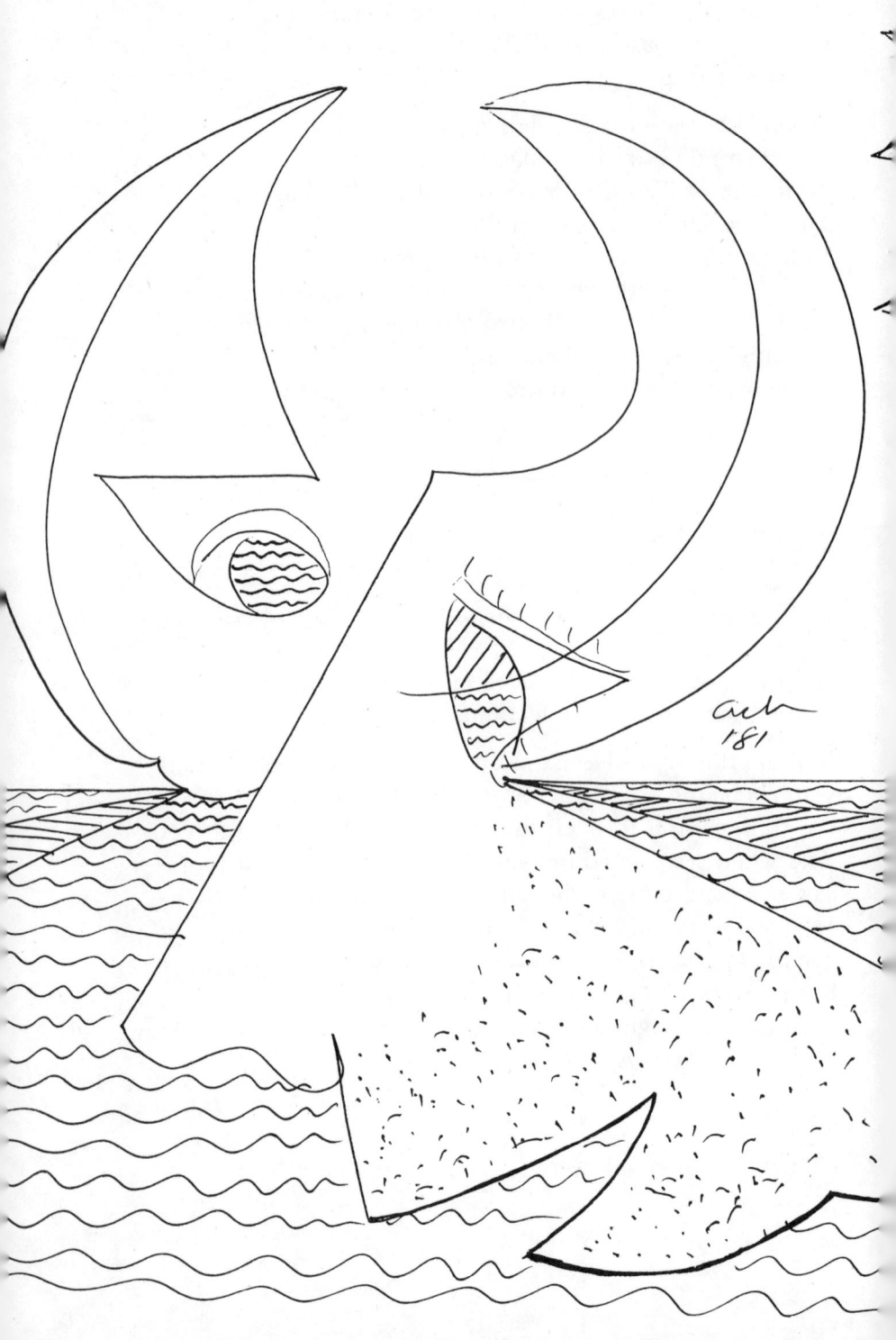

Sgt. Pepper Summer
A Memoir

Now, thirteen and a half years after the fact, they are playing Sgt. Pepper tunes on the radio, part of an hour-long Beatles retrospective on Minneapolis Educational Radio. When Sgt. Pepper came out, though, in 1967, you couldn't hear it on the radio. You had to be at someone's house where it was being played. Sgt. Pepper for me was a kind of communal experience, and was almost a rallying point for an underground of young people from middle class America who were ready to break out into their own world, who were innocent and optimistic.

My brother's apartment was the first place I heard Sgt. Pepper. He was living in Mishawaka, Indiana with his second wife, taught grade school, and was about to move to San Francisco. He had a second floor walkup above a drug store on Lincoln Way East. It was early June, a time that can nearly drive you wild from the sheer beauty of early summer along the St. Joseph river that eventually winds north into Lake Michigan. Nothing will ever be that green again. When you're nineteen or twenty it's easy to think you'll live forever. I would be leaving for Italy in the fall, and this summer was the first time I felt really independent.

2

I had decided to be a poet. Of all the crazy things to do in America, the one profession that seems doomed to almost certain failure is poetry. I was nineteen years old at the beginning of the summer, had read poetry during my two years as a business major at a little Catholic college in Austin, Texas and, while my grades in Marketing and Accounting went down, I wrote poems. For the most part they were failures. Still, a couple were published in the school "literary" magazine and I had even written a sonnet for an English class designed for business majors. While my classmates sat in the library with a collection of Shakespeare's sonnets and tried to plug words into the formula, I wrote a poem that had fourteen lines, loose meter and a few rimes, wrote a justification for a new sonnet form, and handed it in. The next day my teacher wanted to see me in his office. It was a lousy sonnet, he said, terrible. But as a poem, he said, it had promise, and he went on to give it a critique. The first one I ever had.

I knew it was impossible. I thought I would write poetry on the side and do something to make a living. Then Chief, a priest whose name was actually Father Athenasius, a burly man in white cassock and red face, told me that if I didn't become a poet he would kick my ass. At nineteen years old it's hard to know anything other than what one has been told. But I knew, with that innocent optimism, that yes, dammit, I wanted to be a poet, and I was against the war in Viet Nam.

3

A whole generation was deciding it was not happy with the war in Viet Nam. The summer of '67 actually began that spring at the University of Texas in downtown Austin where I began flexing my independence by breaking dorm regulations and stayed out all night at the Wee Hours Club on Red River, listening to a woman named Cairo play rhythm and blues on the funky piano, while hustlers with their johns moved back and forth across the dance floor. There were poetry readings and love-ins sponsored by the SDS. People I never met before would tell me that I had to read Rilke and Rimbaud, the 2 Rs of poetry. Later I'd see Ginsberg read at the bandshell. He'd say how LSD helped get people off heroin and cured alcoholism. He read Wichita Vortex Sutra, a new poem then, and one that still seems, 13 years later, "relevant". "Relevant" was a new word. Life magazine ran a special on people looking for "relevance" in their lives. A picture of a woman who went out at five a.m. in New York City because the city was deserted and she could maybe find herself. At a love-in, a girl told me she ate a rose that day and it was beautiful. When I kissed her, she said thank-you. I had just broken up with Cheryl. We went together through winter and half of that spring, and maybe if we were going together now we would stay together, but those were times of drifting, of incense and marajuana smoke drifting over the campus and the students, trying to say that Austin, Texas could be the San Francisco of the South West.

4

In early June, on a whim, I drove all night and all day from Austin to Indiana in a green '55 Studebaker. The next day I visited Ilych at the I.U. campus in Mishawaka. He said why not go to Italy with him that fall. It was a surprising question, but I had prepared myself for leaving the country earlier that spring, though I didn't know how, or where. It was that kind of trust in the unknown that marked the generation. So it didn't take long for me to say, sure, I'll go to Italy. That was when I went to visit my brother, Ed, who was in many ways my literary mentor. His apartment was six blocks away from where I met Ilych. Sgt. Pepper was playing on the stereo. I had never heard anything like it. It went beyond the first Beatles hits and the haunting tunes of Rubber Soul. Here was subtle politics mingled with surrealism, seeming to call for an internal kind of revolution. New Beatles, with band uniforms and mustaches, and yes, maybe it was possible to go ahead and be a poet. There had never been anything "like" that album, I thought, and maybe there never will again. In any case, there'll never be another summer like that one. There was excitement and newness, even in a town like South Bend where ennui spreads like elms along the river. I'd go home only to sleep. When I got off work I'd eat at McDonald's, a couple of burgers and a shake, meet Frank and Ilych, drop over at Tom L's apartment, go to Pat's farm, neck with Tom's sister, Sharon, for hours on the couch, while Sgt. Pepper played and the others argued politics or philosophy. Once a guy I'd never seen before broke into the argument and pointed me and Sharon out "Look at them, they're the only ones who are doing anything real around here." And Sgt. Pepper went on. After the record was finished, the tone arm would raise automatically, go back to the beginning of the record and start again. I'd stay out until at least two every morning, get up at six, and go to work at the airport. Making a hundred dollars a week, saving for Italy. Sgt. Pepper gave the summer a flavor. A flavor I always hoped I would have at some time in my life. In my nostrils, in the back of my throat. A taste that only music can give, a music that said the Beatles were on our side. A generation that was ready for almost anything new. We were "in between", and my life was about to change in drastic ways—going to Europe, living as an expatriot, learning how to write, burning draft cards. We knew that what we did wouldn't be taken lightly by the establishment, or by our parents. Many of them still can't understand the reasons behind our actions of that spring and summer. And we knew that at some point in the future there would be repercussions to conscientious objections, idealism, going down to Leper park at one thirty in the morning and riding the merry-go-round too fast. But we didn't worry about the repercussions. Musician friends would take up the sitar, people would paint the night sky on their apartment ceilings. We were gong to "expand our consciousness" as much as we could while there was still time.

5

I drove to Muncie for a two and a half day job. On the way back, I stopped in Marion Indiana where an old girlfriend lived. Lani was unique—it was what attracted me to her in the first place—from the way she wore her hair, with a pony tail on the side instead of the back of her head, and the way she talked. We met at a high-school yearbook clinic in Bloomington four years before and stayed in touch off and on though I hadn't seen her for about a year, I gave her a call. She was living with her parents and invited me over for sunday dinner. Her father, who at one time she adored, said that if he knew anyone who would go to Canada rather than serve in the armed forces in Viet Nam, he'd take his shot gun and kill him right there. Lani argued with him, but he was intransigent. I didn't tell them that while I wasn't going to Canada, I certainly wasn't going to Viet Nam. After dinner, Lani took me to the recreation room and played "She's Leaving Home" on the family record player. Quietly, so she wouldn't be overheard, told me that she would be leaving home shortly. Going to Italy of all places—Florence. For a brief moment it seemed everyone was going in the same direction.

6

Today I read a long article about John Lennon in the paper. How he's been a house husband for the past five years, how Yoko saved him from committing suicide by alcohol and drugs. How he has grown up from his days with the Beatles.

After Sgt. Pepper, the Beatles didn't have quite as much impact for me. One winter, when we lived on a farm, some friends brought over Abby Road. "Here comes the sun" was marvelously ritualistic, and because winter still hadn't run its course, had optimism and certainty. But it wasn't Sgt. Pepper. It didn't have that flavor. I can't blame the Beatles, though. If they never did anything again, it would be alright, they had already done enough in 1967, Sgt. Pepper summer, with the draft board looming over everyone. Ilych and I got to New York in early September, at five in the morning, got lost in Harlem, and finally arrived in Greenwich Village, where my friend John was waiting for us under the arch at Washington Square Park. We stayed with him a few days in his apartment on Waverly Place before boarding the DC 7 for Iceland and Luxembourg with our one-way tickets. I sold the Studebaker to a Jehovah's Witness, and Carlos, John's roommate, came in one afternoon with a new record, saying we had to listen to it, it was fantastic, it was Sgt. Pepper.

7

It began and ended the summer. Lucy in the Sky, Fixing a Hole, A Little Help from My Friends, coming out of that apartment in Greenwich Village.

It would be years before I heard it again. It was a record that would bring instant nostalgia, even the first time you heard it. A year later, heads would be busted at the Democratic Convention. The SDS would stockpile guns and TNT and form the Weather Underground. There would be no more love-ins. Janis would die, Kerouac would die. Sgt. Pepper, which was a way people communicated with each other once, would pass into history until tonight when I heard some of the songs again. And with the mind of a realist I thought that no one will ever be able to recreate that era again. With my other mind I know it is waiting to be recreated, and possibly is in the process of being recreated right now, somewhere, among people who still have that kind of innocence— though I won't be part of it.

Later, I would associate other flavors with other times and

events. Some of them I wouldn't realize were possible, if only because I didn't suspect they existed. And there are other kinds of music that I'll carry with me to my grave as well. Each in its own taste slot. Some of them have equalled the intensity and freedom of Sgt. Pepper Summer, and I'll have learned that the depth of human love goes well beyond what I ever imagined. And there are varieties of ecstasy which, for all the pain and boredom we go through, make it possible to still go on. There remain the music, and the tastes, of Sgt. Pepper Summer. An innocence where we were able to stop and look at each other and at ourselves, while we were still the same, and liked what we saw.

8

Epilogue

Today it is the 9th of December, a month after I wrote the above. Last night, Howard Cosell who, it is nearly ironic, has considerable sensitivity, broke in during the play by play of Monday Night Football and said we have to remember that in spite of play-off hopes, this is just another football game, and in the face of a tragic event is rather insignificant. John Lennon was just gunned down outside his apartment, and was dead on arrival. Today the whole world knows. An impromptu shrine on the apartment house gate. Crowds of mourners. The morning news full of experts, music critics, old D.J.s. I told Gaylord about it this morning when he stopped over. Said I wouldn't be working today. Gaylord hadn't heard about Lennon yet. He just sat there and said "you've got to be kidding." No reason for it—some psychotic with a .38 emptied the chamber in his back.

Later, I sit back and put on an old scratched copy of Sgt. Pepper that belongs to a friend. It must have been played a million times. There is nothing more to say beyond those last words, "I'd love to turn you on", the resolving piano chord dissolving, allowed to decompose, the scratches and pops as the needle settles into the final groove, and goes on like that for a few minutes. I don't feel like I have the energy to get up and take the record off. Meanwhile, people are still standing around the apartment building in New

York, about a thousand of them, the news says, singing "Give Peace a Chance", and the radio stations begin playing all the tunes they wouldn't touch in 1967.

Enlightenment Comes Yesterday

It is already October 3, everyone has finished a September poem but me. It was hot but not remarkable. In the school rooms the varnish began to swell and mingle with children's sweat. Leave alone the facts—that September turns the corner to complete the square of the year, or that the ninth month wears the holy number seven.
It is beyond me, this secondary algebra of the seasons, and this city with its clocktower at high noon, the people drifting through the park —it could be September now but what do I know— a man stands behind me taking pictures, people do not talk. A quick black shape flits before me in downtown St. Paul just like it would in September if September were important. It is not September because so many people have cameras. And the man who sells hot dogs from his little truck on the far curb doesn't have much business today. He's as hooked on the smells of the city as everyone else. He sits just before lunch hour under the mountain ash in a lawnchair. Nothing bothers him, not even me walking up for a cup of coffee. I could go into the tiny kitchen, draw the cup of coffee, leave thirty cents in the change tray but it would disturb the ecology of the moment. He would leave immediately for Arizona instead of waiting for the first snow. I have seen the old man with him more now, and the woman also, in the cab of the truck or on a second green lawn chair. A fine silence connects them to the air we breathe and the fountain that runs dry in the center of the park. Each knows the futility of speaking. Would just as soon ask the leaves to understand their pain in having to turn again green under the blue skies when this is all the ecstasy we'll ever need. Would sooner say enlightenment comes yesterday.

III

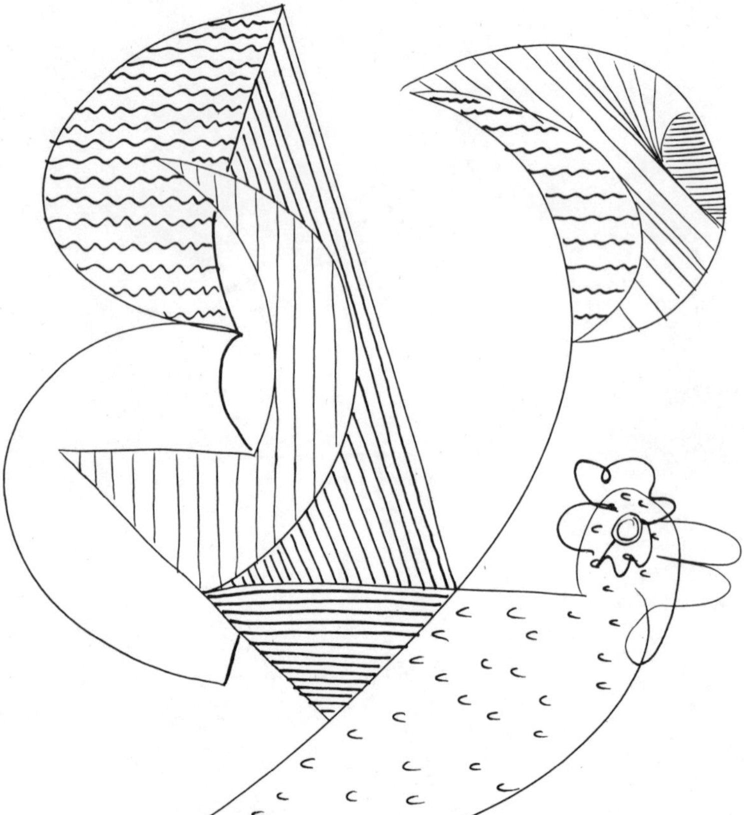

The Shot Gun of Desire

for Art Pepper

It's more than time for hyacinths
that breathe under blossoms of snow.
Every night the dragons of the moon
strain at black reins. Every day
the shot gun of desire lets go its round
and we have albino bees stampeding
into the distant mouth of august
who sits on a stump with his shirt off.

Outside, a robin pauses with a twig
in its mouth, presses down
the snow, and thinks it is only
the beginning of eggs.
No rest. Press the snow.
There are worms down there
farming the clay.

Try to answer
the questions posed by snow.
Why should those tracks go anywhere,
you say, we all come from the sun.
But snow is like a child. It keeps asking
the same questions, wanting the same answers.
Wants you to write something
on it before it melts. It wants you to think
of a Japanese woman who spent five hours
powdering her face before coming to see you.
And then it melts, falls off branches
and leaves snake-like etchings on the ground.
It doesn't need you after all.

Palm Sunday

The sermon goes on all week—
Came in town on a donkey
like the fresh fruit express
rolling into the station
while snow kept melting
and a little volcano erupted
in my ten-year-old daughter
all day, day of palms. And
it is still March, a mechanical
turtle of a month, going front-
ward, back, colliding with
the wall, veering
off again. Snow, rain
melt, flood, the clouds gasp
and yawn over the full moon.
Grackles arrive in the still naked
trees and brown grass.

The speed of light is as refreshing
as the existence of tortillas.
For the 33rd time I announce
that the snow is gone.
We welcome the invader with
open arms, we wave branches
in the wind, announcing we,
the survivors, surrender.

And March lays down its weapons.
How sad it is . . . it bites
its tongue, doesn't wave,
looks back with big eyes,
moves off
like the sultan's favorite wife
learning she has been replaced.

The Photographs

Three doors converge in the corner of this room. All are open. One is pink, one yellow, one white. Some days I wish I were a photographer so I could record their shadows falling across each other or the diagonal of sunlight on the white one, reflecting on the dark side of the pink one, faintly illuminating the yellow, the one that always stands in the shadow.

I have photographed others — doors leading to more doors where the last door, the closet one, was slightly open, and behind it the darkness that went forever.

If you put a child in a closet and hold your foot against the door he will grow up never being able to run fast enough up the dark basement stairs because any second the stairs will begin treadmilling backwards and all is lost. The basement is always dark when he leaves it and the cut back winter plants, the tools, voices we think belong to someone else but are really our own.

Lock a child in a closet and you will have a convert to mysticism, and a belief in the darkness we wear behind the faces we cannot live without.

There are enough beautiful things in this world — the gardens, the dogs who rest their warm chins against our legs in winter. Then our mothers, with the faces we always feared they would have shove us into the dark closet, and we think we can endure this absence of light until our fathers or brothers who were waiting behind the empty suitcases and old coats begin moaning and reach out for our legs, our hair — and we, who were so comfortable being alone, cannot bear this knowledge there are secret doors leading to other doors. . . .

So we turn the handle and step out again into the room, fresh air, light, and there is no one to hold us, nothing, only three doors in the corner, and three door knobs like a pointillist painting, staring into different directions, and photographs whose messages are hidden, that line the bottoms of drawers, silent, pretending they'll never be found.

Lost White Brother in Rome

There are days I would wake up if the rain would stop for more than two hours. It is like the bars we left behind on via degli Angeli Bruni, the girls whose fingers fell limp over our shoulders and asked for the local champagne. Dogs were barking when we left. Smoke rose from the river.

We were going down via del Corso in the rain and stopped at a music shop for you to write something on the clip board you always had with you, and for me to ask the man, slowly, if they had any bassoons. You carried the weight of ink with you. I, as usual, was empty handed.

Now the sun is rising over Vittorio Emmanuelle. I have been awake all night again and remember trying to decipher the look in your eyes when you narrowed them and told me I was mad.

I suppose I told you about waiting for Angelica on a foggy night in February on Ponte Mazzoni, and the old man who watched the river wanted to hold my arm. His mustache pointed down to the brown water. *Don't jump.* Angelica that night told me I was politically immature— we kissed before she got into a cab and disappeared forever by the post office in the blur of a green and yellow Fiat.

John, what can match the darkness of this night. I left you standing too many times with a confused look on your face at the Rome Airport. I have gone back to learning the drum and can't say why. I listen to the slow march of tablas across a marsh in the burning sun. The animals silent and gathered. I fear I am training for greater emergencies.

The Invention of Weather

It was like our mothers looking for us
with a switch, a pair of pants,
a suitcase. Their expressions of terror,
seeing our faces

smeared with grease from cars' chassis.
They came with a rag, holding
a broom in both hands
scattering stray dogs as if destiny

is the shape of a run-over tricycle.
The rain mothers stand close
to the idea of an empty grave
listening as our voices call for rain.

It drives toward its *own* beginnings
like a clock that runs in reverse.
Like the invention of memory, the accumulating
gerontometer, the black box, first thing

rain seeks when one of our lives end.
Like the invention of dreams and the smoky wings
that brush our faces as we sleep;
a fine rain of sun begins to fall.

The Language of Animals

A cold day in Minnesota.
The ripples of winter and spring
reach out and touch
like the large moon
rising directly ahead

with the expression of a mother
holding her dead son.
My dog plays with an old shoe
as if it is still animal
still alive.

I put whale music on the record player. It would be nice
to take my tongue
and see what else it needs
to speak the language of animals.

In the yard the dog runs ahead
like an eel
twisting through high grass.
She circles back.
She barks

as if to say
follow her
through the budding trees
where the light I cannot see
shines like swamp gas.

I laugh. She stops, turns
to face me. How can I
protect her from death now
now that her ears have picked up
its faint music.

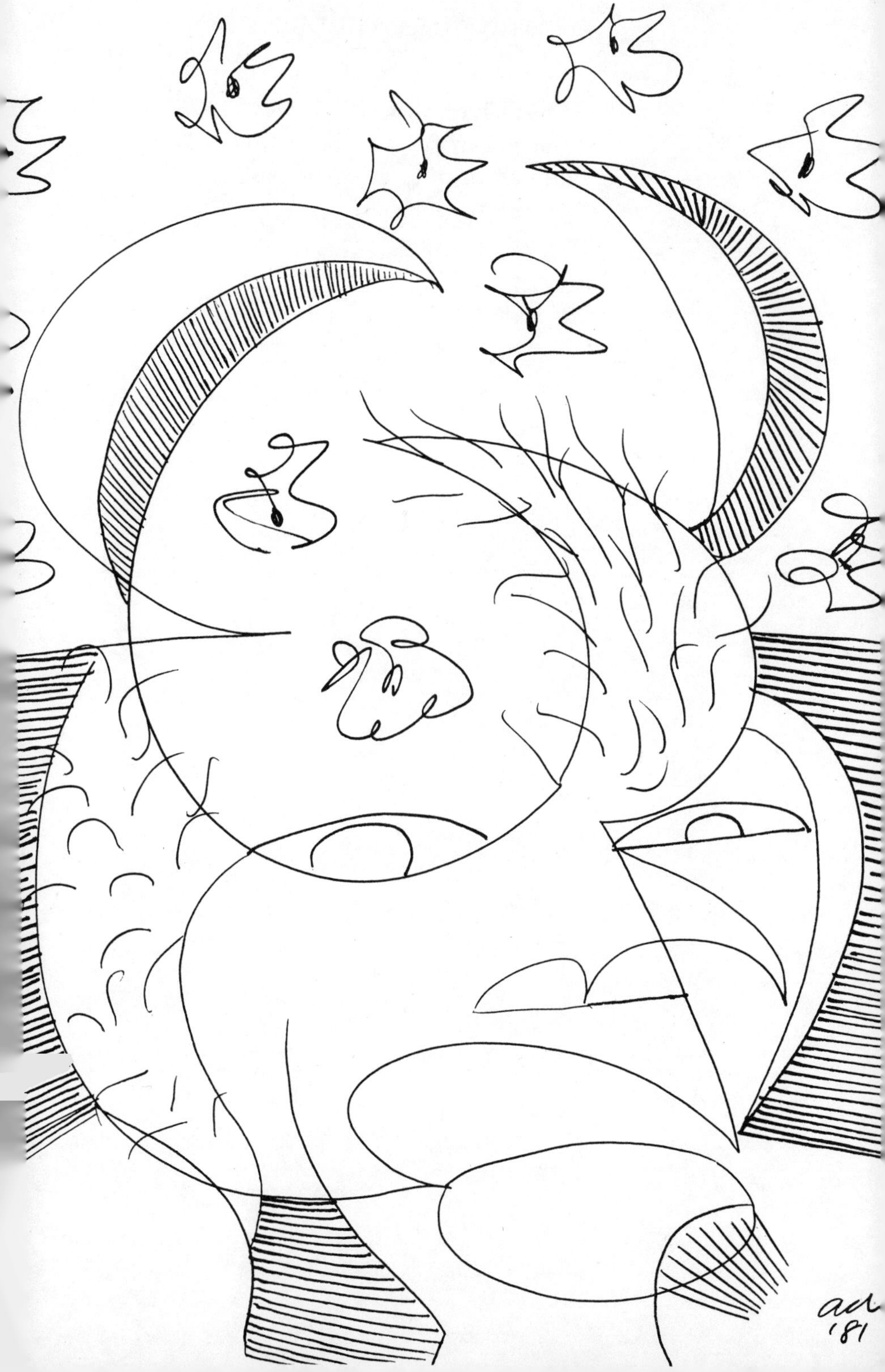
ad
'81

Nice Serpent

I want both to feed
and to satisfy. While crawling
among peoples' feet, I choose
yours to curl around.

Nice serpent, you say
as I coil up your leg,
the left one, and show
you the real reason
for a forked tongue.

Snake Man in Winter

I do not want to hold anyone at the moment.
It is not the long nights that matter so much
it is the waiting for eye to meet eye,
for me to say

I am afraid I love you too much.
Don't you hear guitars in the distance?
I confess I am in love with your spleen.
Let me show you what it was like
being in Piazza Navona in 1968
in the dense fog at 3 am, the belfry
leaning two inches over the statue
of the triton . . .

Let me buy you fine dresses.
Have you seen Barcelona in the spring?

You smile knowingly, clutch
your shopping bag closer. There is
a true distance in your eyes as you
amble toward your car, your house.
You'll open
your child's encyclopedia and look up
Barcelona; the view overlooking
Gaudi's apartment building. You'll feel
as if there's an avocado pit in your stomach.

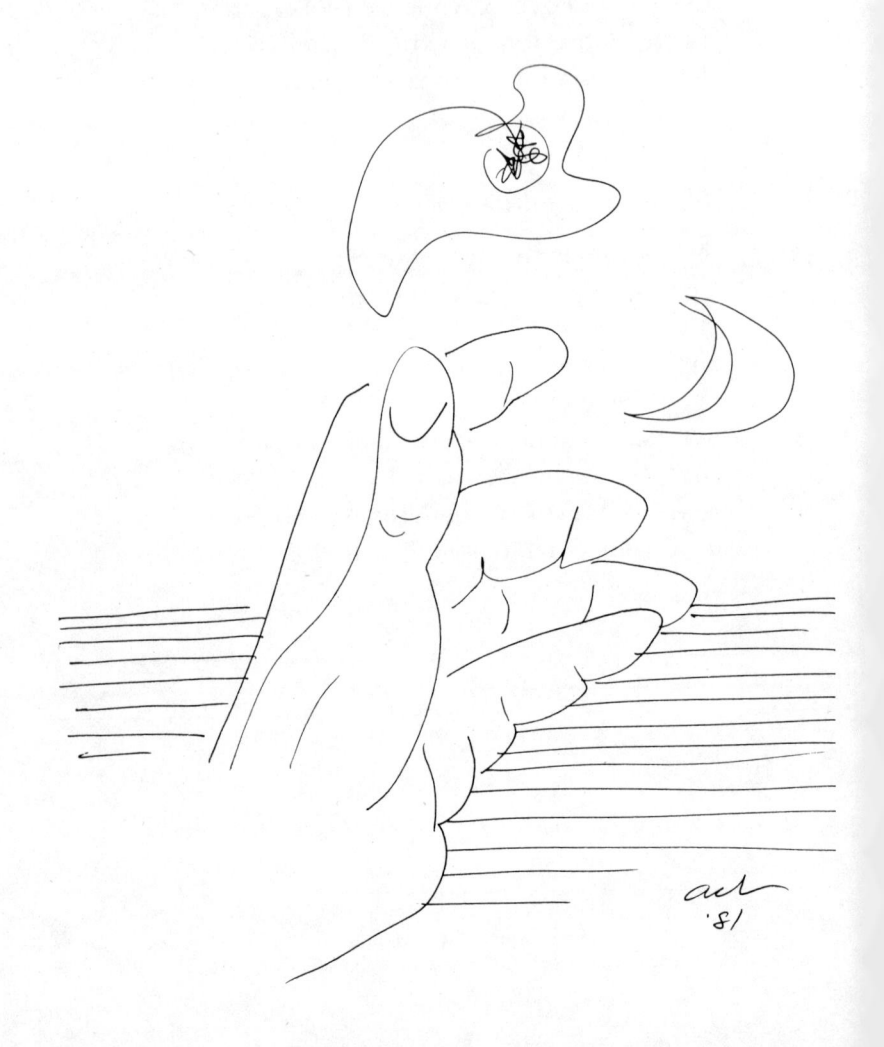

To Measure the Hand

The night freight rolls south
like a caravan of pigeons lost in the desert
looking for a fragrant patch of soil.

It is enough to watch your hands
as you pour another glass of wine
in this hotel where the elevator wheezes
all night

like an old man dreaming of the cauldron
his children push him nearer. You talk
about violent water pipes that jolt you
out of bed at 5 am. I know

there's a price to lips, the dense waves
that roll back from the future.

You hold your arms above your head like feathers
waiting for the still invisible spring
to draw closer and look for your hand,
the right one — the umbrella.

The train presses on toward some town
and the cows sleeping beside the road
have staked out the territory
they will abandon come high water.

The wind marches around buildings carrying
rainbows of snow, luminescent as peaches
floating through neon.

The Moon's Scars

It was so cold machetes could be honed on your skin.
You crossed the street and sat down
in the pool of light from the corner grocery.
There wasn't an ounce of moon in the brittle sky.

I roll down my window — your sobbing comes thick
in the wind and blows through South Minneapolis.

I want to drive you somewhere. You tuck your head
against your knees and shake it. Cars
are stopped around us. They have seen movies
of explorers who fell asleep in a snow drift
and never woke again. Three hours from now
no one would bother you as if there's a cure

for sadness, here, on the concrete,
the stoplight flashing green, red, yellow above you.

A man who looks like he might remember your name
is talking to you. You say — "Thank you".
I drive with the radio off. The moon's scars
never heal. Another car goes around the block

a second time. This is Minneapolis, thank you,
this is thirty-fifth around the corner
where Ramona lived, thank you, who is back east
and somewhere tonight there is a warm bed—
do not say I never loved you.

Snake Eyes

I have risen from the basket like a rope.
It must be something in the air, like music—
to be influenced by music alone
not the motion of the musician.

How small my eyes look to you — ridiculous
too small eyes on a slender stalk.
When you glance toward me quickly
after watching a man with a saxophone

There are waves & islanders dancing.
Speech hinders us!
Hypnosis is a two way street with pale lamp posts
after a hard rain. A fine mist rises

out of the paving just as night
clicks shut its tiny castanets.
The knife is under the table between us.
The ship with the chief's body drifts out, burning.

Snake to His Lost Love

Rain in Louisiana, we meet in high water.
It is mid-june, you stand on a table
in the yard while the sky boils up grey.
Your father is out in his pirogue.
I am looking for high land. You lean
against your mother

ask for the thousandth time why they're called
cottonmouths. You know it looks
soft, like cotton, and through your terror,
almost feel like testing the lightning
in my mouth.

I watch only you. It is 1929. There is a depression,
a flood is happening. Your father is rowing toward the house,
he is tired from saving people all day,
like Noah who already has two of everything.
The water licks your feet. You are about
to hear my voice in your head as the oar
comes down again, and again
and I make my way slowly to another world.
My only hope is that something I said stayed with you
that you'll forgive me for not going as far as I could.

In another life it would have been different.
I would be the butterfly perched on your shoulder.
You'd wonder if I glowed in the dark. Now
there is just this trail of blood and the winding
motion through water. You know I will grow
another head, another tail. You will spend
the rest of your life waiting for me,
while I choose any convenient tree to rest in,
and call, and call across the water.

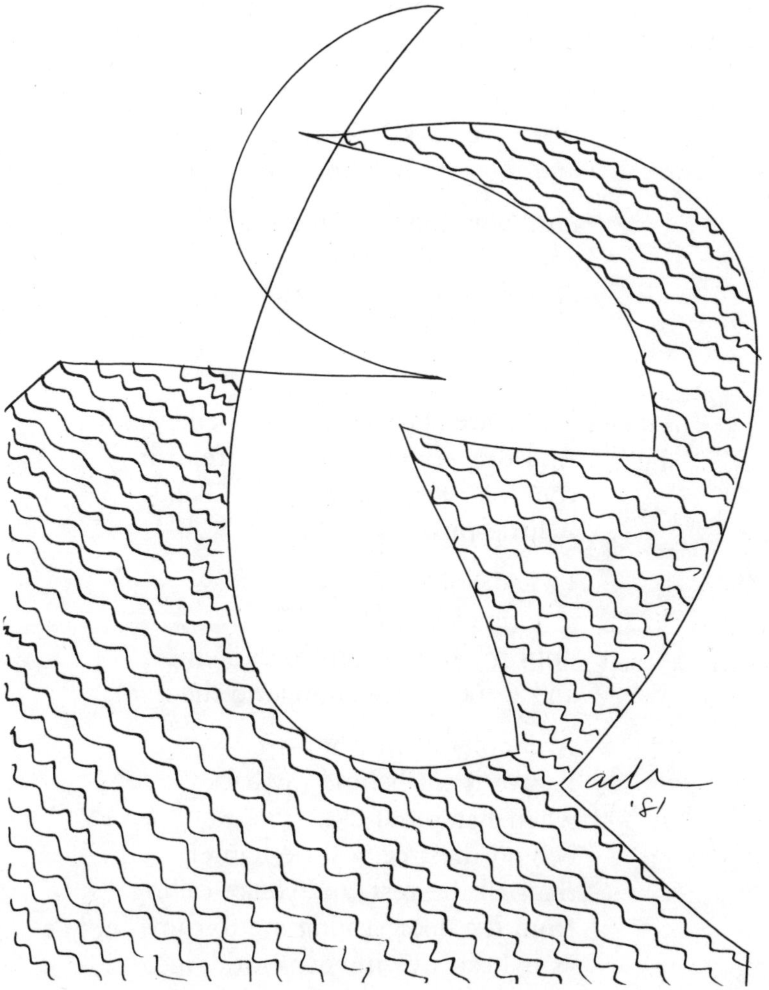
'81

Five Nocturnes

for my daughter

I

We got back from the post offiice
in a night so dark
you ran straight to the house
for the little solace of light.

I stayed out back between two elms.
Darkness so complete only my skin
kept me from joining it.

You can never turn completely
from the dark. It sneaks up
and rests its hand on your shoulder

until you, too, love the night
and are a little afraid
of what you love.

II

There are stars that look friendly.
And though you're not aware of it
you hold something in your hand:
A little piece of night.

I could hold it for you
as long as you like, or
until my face begins to darken
and I drag my shadow into the light.

An apple. A blossom.
I wave them behind my back
when I step out
behind the tree, a little lighter
than all the rest, and you're calling
from the door, asking me to come in,
as if I can live in your world, too.

III

A shot.
I sit upright in bed
bolt downstairs
and you're waiting
revolver in your hand.

I sit on the bottom stair
you walk to me slowly
cock the pistol
hand it to me
like a fish
tail first.

I aim at your head
while you watch carefully.

Everytime there is a door
we have to knock
and go in.

I am not Abraham
no angel comes to stop us
I squeeze the trigger
the gun does not fire
and between us is all this silence
as if nothing has happened.

There is a long corridor of doors
            before us now
the streets of heaven
are paved with them
and we say nothing
about thinking
we were beyond this
as we hug in the still morning
of the first test.

IV

We arrived in the drizzles of March
to a different Rome than the one I knew,
it was like the City had just been planted
but it was still Rome along the mud-caked
streets, along the river.

A man and a woman came to our hut
and took us to a restaurant
in a cave by the Tiber. Smoke from the candles
added another shade of black to the ceiling
where strings of onion and garlic hung
like great nautical ropes.

The waiter stood beside us
as people came from the dark interior
of the cave and took shape.

How could we remember all their names.
They were like shadows. Or the dead—the friendly dead.

I wanted to tell you not to be afraid
and teach you certain songs
but I'm not sure if I brought you here
or you brought me—the table
grown suddenly long
to accomodate the silent, smiling dead.

Just yesterday you said
we are like each other:
Same long legs, same long fingers.
Each of us has one eye that's
like a messenger with a slight stoop

and we're in the middle of a crossroads,
deeper than the caves of language
where we ask no questions of the dead.

Their gifts are lined up on the table.
By the time we go back
they'll have grown immensely small.
We are born for finding our way home in the dark.

V

It is dawn — you are already awake.
I am going to sleep, having been up all night.
There are songs for waking up and going to sleep
that we keep to ourselves.

Your ghosts are leaving you now
and mine are just returning.

Will we always follow each other like this?

IV

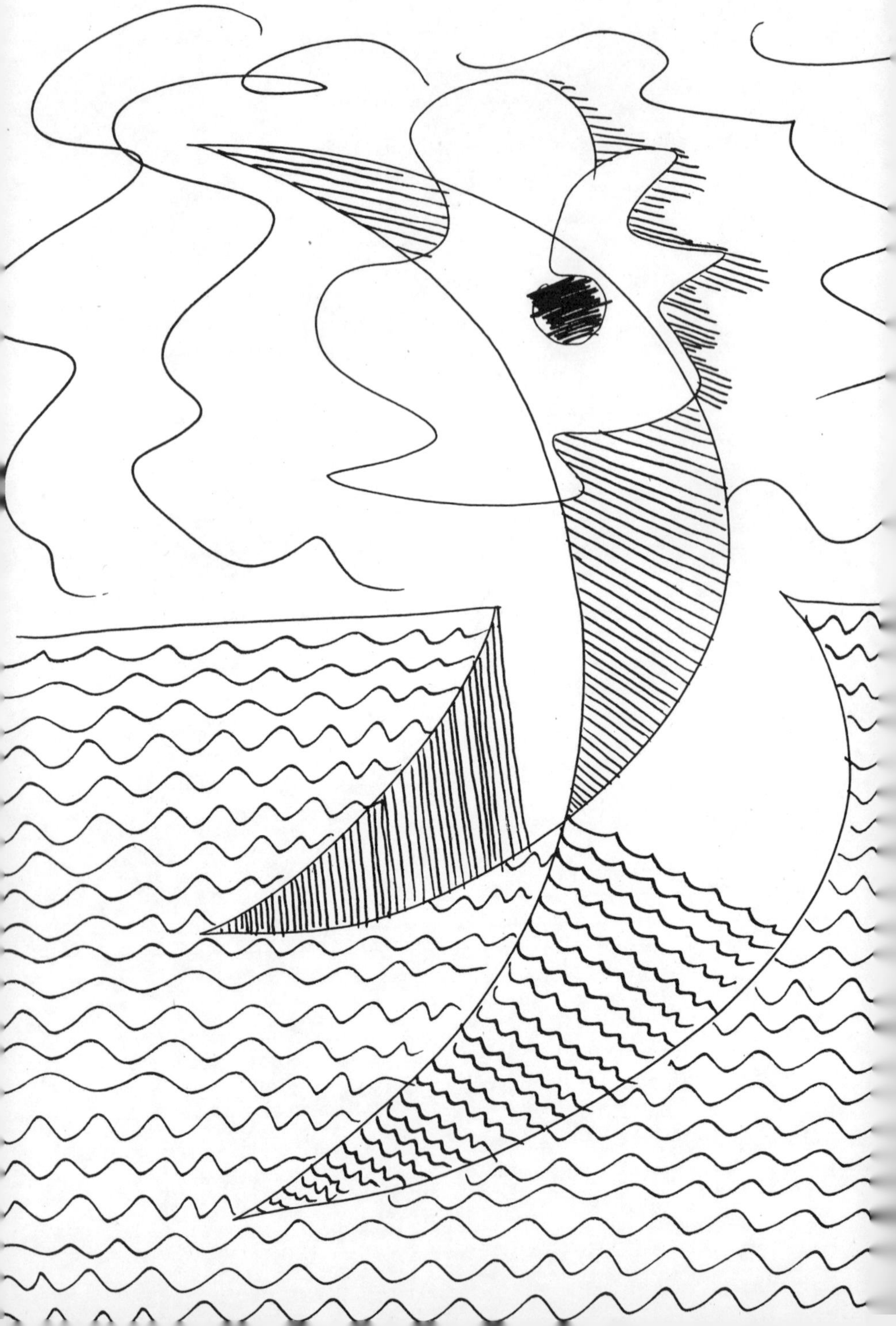

Lot's Wife in the Twentieth Century

Salt was the only cure for tears
so when I turned and saw
every face give over to vapor
I tasted nothing. House, furrow,
each voice gave breath
to flame. What happened to cats
and stone walls — with each
footstep fire sprang.

I found myself on a hill looking
over the valley —echoes—
kitchens gone, carts gone,
camels, loaves, the golden sandals
of the magistrate's daughter.
I turned toward the night, and my husband
is gone, my children gone. Gone ahead
and I follow. The dutiful wife.
The clouds remind me of fish.

Somewhere behind, my mother is buried.
The bracelet on my arm has turned green.
Behind me something is still warm.
All we ever own is this gravity
and this salt, this cauldron of silence.
My children have stopped talking —
they go into a different kind of fire.
Hand me the spade. We are given this land.
It is the only thing that owns us.

I remember red dresses, how the women
opened their mouths as if praying. Black
roofs. The orange gardens.
Monkeys pulled organ grinders
down the street. They were
serious with destinations of their own.
Miners in the bars raised their glasses calmly
their faces illumined and tender.

I turned and the road ahead was empty.
The stars behind the clouds rode down
the north. Waves. I almost wish I rode
beneath the sea. I heard a song once —
how clouds make the sky less crowded but no
less empty. Even stars, they tell us,
drift apart. I chose to turn around.
To see the baker climb to the top of the stairs
with a load of cinders on a wooden board.

And flame spurted from the eye of rhododendrons
and the cruel irises. From key holes.
Flame erupted in the street of harlots.
Navels glowed red, diamonds melted.
When someone turns back, it is the woman
who pays. People say this was Lot's wife,
this, Eurydice. The past flows through
us. I walk thinking of the sea
the waters of the beginning, to wash sand

out of my hair. The wise man seeks the sea.
The man who wants to be wise seeks the mountain.
I only walk. There is only the destination
I carry inside me, only the starvation of shells
across the desert, lost hitchhikers, merchants
of sand who ate gold flakes in their food
instead of salt, the simplicity of donkeys
outside our house in summer, trenches, charred water.

I think of a ship, of a diamond in my pocket, my husband.
What journey, I said. Don't ask, he said. I packed
dried dates and a fish. I tied a scarf on my neck.
Afternoon filled the town, a man selling umbrellas
crossed the square for a place to lie down. Plums
were bursting on the trees. A scrawny boy looked
up at the window of the girl he loved. I almost want
to become a moth. I turned my head forward again.
I said to my husband, giving him the baby, "you go on."

Let someone else poke through the ruins and lie
in them, put their ears to the ground and listen for gold.
Every star was a diamond once. A woman has had enough fire.
My arms grainy with salt. When the smoke cleared,
no light shone, no moon. No being on the road.
Then stars, one by one. I obeyed in every respect but one.
I might learn to live with this taste on my lips.
I put one foot in front of the other, following in my time,
Lot. How I almost drowned in that name.

Wild Rose

*After Sonny Rollins
for Seraphim Minczewski*

I can almost hear the words
in the snow and weeping that comes
from a warm place though I've long
given up saying where that is
and in something as cold
as Minnesota tonight
there is a door
in this music that lets in no drafts,
that says there are 99 steps
on the stairway to heaven
and 99 years to climb them,
inhaling the smoke of our ancestors
the fields of Seraphim,
a wild rose like dusk
that indirect color after love
among the sun's dynasties,
another thing born without wings.

Name of the Muse

for Rene Boreades

1. Autobiography

Old. She lingered in the chair
waiting for me to wake up.
The moon was high, shadows
of elms filtered into the room
like samovars lying on their sides.
I was dreaming of her, her coarse babushka
while she sat there making sure
my eyes were open before fading
into the rest of the night.

It was the way she looked at me
and my sudden horror at a second mother.
If I could talk then, I'd ask
what she was doing — what news.
Sometimes there were voices in the laundry chute
       help me, help me
and I am nine and pray myself into fevers
and no one is there. Or it is she
with eyes set so deep in her sockets,
I cannot see them.

Old women.
I remind them of their sons.
The beggar in Rome who, finishing her beer
and a smile with no teeth in it,
says Help me to my feet, sonny,
and I heave her up. Hand her crutch
over. It is spring, little ecstasies
are exploding around us and she says
"where are you going now?
You got enough to eat?
A place to stay?"

2. J. S. Bach

There are so many. Bach once told me
the muses used to crowd around him to see what was up.
They would whisper to him —
three voices at once — four voices.
He'd stick his tongue out and touch a breast.
His fingers flew over the clavichord
and those muses did more than just dance.

He liked it just fine — they always wanted more.
And sometimes it was just one who sat beside him,
her ear to his all afternoon, melody after slow melody,
choirboys waiting in the chapel.
She held her finger to his lips
and watched his hands turn it into song.

3. Apotheosis

Erato, Thalia are just ghosts
just ghost names we go seeking
at night along dusty hallways
behind doors with creaky latches.
You enter, the candle flickers
but stays lit. There are no names
for the ancient woman applying makeup
before her mirror.

You could have been more patient, you tell yourself.
Her lips tighten, a faint smile
*Why honey , I didn't know you liked me
as I really am.*

Forgive her, she has no name.
Only ghosts of names
fluttering about her head.
Forgive the minutes
that have fallen asleep in her lap
and dream of the present.

She rises, her skin
looses its pallor,
she opens a door
Give me a minute baby ,
you can wait in here.

There are photographs of you in the other room,
of you and her on the beach at Lake Michigan,
in the gardens of Spoleto.

You are about to open the book of your life
that's sitting on the table
when you are aware of her fragrance.
She stands by the door, ready,
younger, and drifts toward you.

Hand in hand you sneak downstairs
avoid the loud party in the dining room
and escape into the night,
the deserted streets,
her twin sisters waiting.

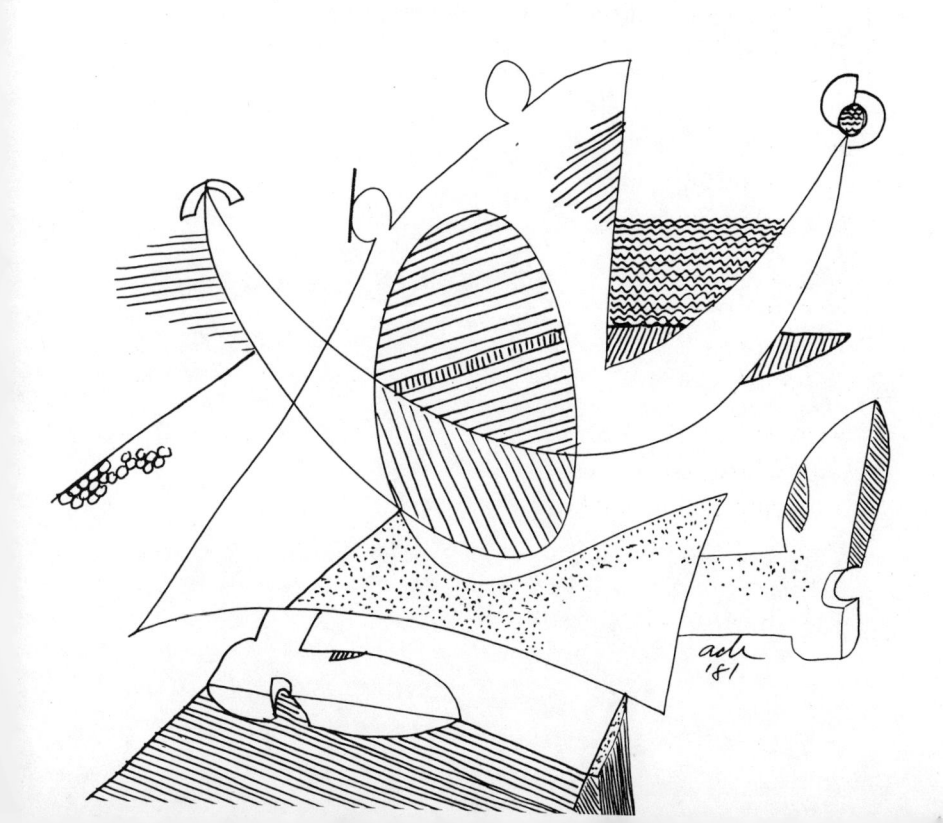

Old Ego Song

Old ego climbing out of the trap door on the top of my head.
Wearing his bald ego feathers, strutting around the house,
turning lights off and on. Bald ego stepping out
to pick up another pack of cigarettes —flying high—
ego-eyed.

Old ego coming back from the grocery store, climbing back
in through the trap-door, thinks he's 30 years old, thinks
he really knows how to tune up a Volkswagon. He even thinks
he can dance alright though we all know better.

Old ego sitting down in his chair thinking back
on what happened this morning, thankful he turned down
the newspaper job.

He should be out grilling steaks in the backyard.
He should be eating meat. But he's just chuckling to himself
and he's not saying what it is.

I suppose we should leave him there, alone,
nodding off to sleep, dreaming.

Vivaldi Lives

Vivaldi lives, and Bach lives,
under the basement stairs
in an old closet.

There is little left to surprise them
but all night they listen
to whatever sounds come their way.

A slow night freight three blocks off.
They raise their hands
over their sad faces,
begin conducting.

Poland: Current Events

Chopin, as a boy, loved the sight of rainbows.
He built one out of playing cards
he found in his father's underwear drawer.
When the rainbow was complete, he said
"On this side stands Chopin."

He flew over the rainbow of cards.
"I stand on this side," he laughed.

Oh, what can the trees do, who can hold
in his palms the cup of the sun and not spill?

The teacher, in his blue suit
paces the study, recites lessons
to no one. Poor little Chopin.
Let us carry him to bed.
No one holds the sun.
There is nothing more the trees can do.

The Invention of Silence

When they handed Chopin a bagpipe
and took his piano away
he looked at the woman he loved
wearing a mauve gown
sitting across the room
by the window. She was reading.
He thought she would need
glasses within the year—
she was already forgetting
what he looked like.

He glanced down at his hands,
his fingers covering the stops
of the chanter. Already
the drones were beginning to squeak
from the hushed air
inside them.

This is how silence mends itself,
he thought, as if this were the answer
to the silence piled up
at the edge of our knowing.

A flock of crows rises in the distance
like old boatmen casting off.

Stop, dearest, she cries,
you will give yourself
another hemorrhage.

Ah, this is bitter honey
he tells himself. The drones
slow down and melt.
He waits for the old spasm
to repeat.
My dear, let me kiss you.

Tzara

for Frank Foulks

It is a sunday and afternoon is raging in the outskirts of Zurich.
Already summer is closing the door on 1916
waiting for the watchman with sealing wax and padlocks.
I don't know what people will say when the seal
is finally broken or if they'll just screw up their faces
and say "what air the people breathed."

And Tristan Tzara is sitting on the park bench with wrought
      iron legs
matching the ironwork on the table in front of him. His foot
rests on the lower rung. The pine tree behind him appears
      to grow out of his head
like the tree we create every night in our sleep.

Thrust out of sight is the newspaper listing the war dead,
Theophile among them, and the notebook
      where he has just written
"I'm leaving to die in a far inn."

Still, his hair falls into place
forming, with his left eyebrow,
the initials of his name
and two long question marks.

A reporter standing next to the photographer asks
"will the public take your new aesthetic seriously,
herr Tzara?"

"The public is serious only about what appears in the papers
and it is the stalest news in the world.
Do you know your own hands? Are your eyes brown?
Whatever you answer is a lie!"

The cameraman sets off the flash powder.

Everything will be washed out in the photo
but the dark suit, hair, park bench,
a few trees in the near background,
pebbles.

"You see," he says, eyes narrowed,
"It is already too late to turn the century around."

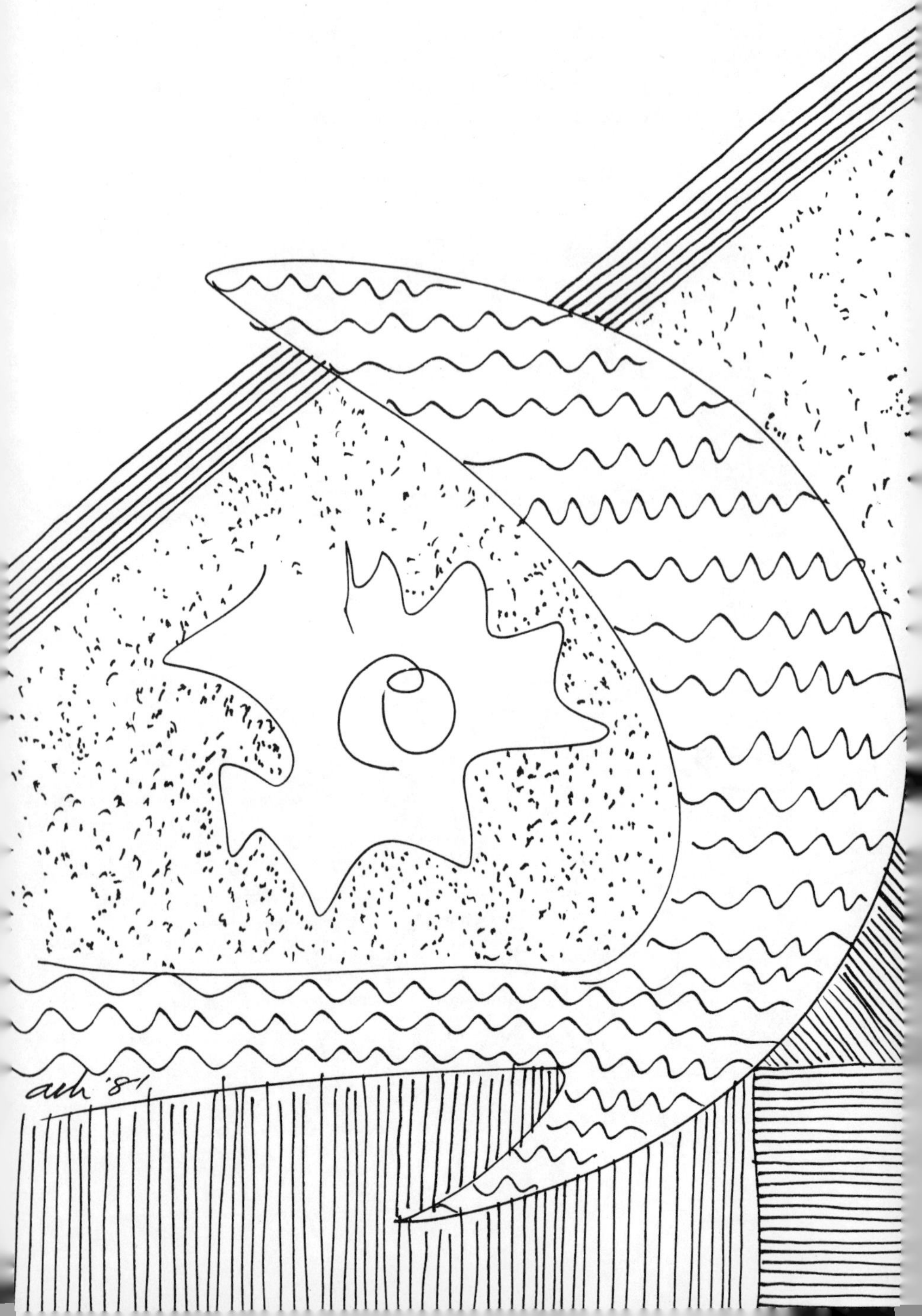
ach '81

The Reconstruction of Light

after Malloch
for Anna Guaita

There was only
the whiteness of objects when Bach died,
and the art of fugue sprang into silence
the way an ocean looks the first time
"Like heaven, so round—like the path
the soul takes." He goes no further than this
and maybe he's gone too far already.

When he blows out the lamp
he has to squint against the brightness
in the room. As if light
has descended, like water—
an element. A shadow is standing
by the window, like smoke, radiating quietly
like an after-image of dusk.

The manuscript page
in Altnikol's lap seems to glow
and blend with the inkwell
on the board across the arms of his chair.
Altnikol, the son-in-law,
sits next to the bed
taking notes. It is plain
Bach has taken his greatest risks
already and made good on them.
And you will get better still, Altnikol exclaims.
Ach, my shadow is breaking away, JB retorts.
He speaks so quietly now. He has become

successful at playing with light,
making chords of the light chorus.
Altnikol takes it down.

Sometimes he thinks he's Beethoven,
or that other "B", Brahms,
that Brahmin Bull of a Brahms.
"B" he says, his mouth folding around the letter.

Altnikol, the last notes falling from his pen,
an expectant look on his face, sees the lips move.
Maestro, please repeat. How often these words
have interrupted as he has lain in bed.
One works hard and it is never hard enough.
Altnikol, Altnikol, I am not the man
with the answers.

The Detective

for Jessica

1. *The Master Sleuth*

A foggy night in London along the wharves.
Footsteps. A tall figure draws his pea
coat tighter about him. The familiar hawk
nose leaves a wake in the air behind Holmes
the master sleuth.

It is midnight, at least. A faint
click of rat nails on the cobbles.
No one will sleep tonight. Before next day-
fall someone will die — we know it
already. The good outnumber the bad
as they always do.

If we don't sit still we'll upset
the balance. Even crunching popcorn
like we do might be heard sometime in the past
by Moriarty and throw him on guard
at the wrong time.

Holmes has taken that into account
as he is led by Moriarty's men to the hideout.
He will allow us to think for a moment
that the bombsight will fall into the wrong
hands, and he will be dumped into the north sea
in the bottom of a carpenter's chest.

If only it would stay illusion
we could turn our backs, unplug the clocks,
pull the blinds, turn off the lights, pretend
England was saved forty years ago.
We will listen in the dark for the furnace

to click on and off, and the November wind blow
outside like a jet taxiing onto the runway.
We are waiting on the other side to make our entrance.

Holmes is in grave danger. He has convinced Moriarty
that his death should be imaginative
and slow. We know he is buying time.

We must be wary of the criminal slipping through our net,
we must act at the right moment — just as Moriarty leaves
the room to join his confederates — Holmes strapped
to the table — ready to let World War II
go to the crackpots.

2. *The Magnifying Glass*

There is only one set of prints on the handle
and the after-image of an eye, enlarged,
like clam-meat, regarding the spot
of dried blood on the carpet. A cold wind outside.
The voice of the detective trails off
the way fog grows out of the river Thames.

An eye glass looks both ways at the same time.
It does not make sense of what it sees.
Its brain, also, does not know what to do
with Holmes' dilating iris as the back of his head
receives a blow from the master criminal.

I knew a man who put clocks into magnifying glasses.
Ingenious hands moving in a tiny circle. In his log
book the entries; "I watched the fingerprints from 12:15
to 12:19 — nothing." "Nov. 17, 1936: Her lips made small
droplets of moisture on the lens. I came so near waking her.

I left through the dumb waiter as usual."
It is not crystal, it cannot fortell the future,
it is a lousy flier, it becomes easily fixed
on whatever it sees — in this case the pocket
of Sherlock Holmes who is now effecting his escape
under the hot lights of the movie studio.

It is asleep now, dreaming vaguely of checkered hats,
of the sea, of heat we cannot imagine. It hopes
it will never see another eye. For there are no victims,

it thinks, there are no saviors, no master criminals.
And jail is the safest spot in the world.

3. *Closing the Net*

A rosy dust settles on everything.
Maybe it doesn't have to be rose.
It could be the lights dancing up
when we forget how long the night
has become. If we could just
break into song now, if it weren't

forbidden to break the deep well of silence
as we lose the days of November.
Put a pillow on the telephone
let nothing mar the perfect death
Holmes has planned for Moriarty.

Tell yourself this is just a movie
and there'll always be an England.
The sun strikes the lower corner of the sky.
A sudden realization strikes Moriarty's eyes
as he falls through the trap door he designed
against enemies like Holmes who edges into view
             around the opening.

Dawn and the detective's eyes look heavy.
He has lost the only man he could ever love.
They were molded together in the danger
they created for each other, while bombs
go on dropping on Charing Cross Station.

Next morning men wait in line outside
the Union Jack Hotel. You can have your pick of them
though they're old now with some terrible secret
they hold back. And we go back to the silence
at the end of the film —the ur-music, light,
like a new moon— serene: gold, silver, opium, cocaine.

Circle Routes

Akron Series in Poetry

Winner of the 2000 Akron Poetry Prize

ALSO BY JOHN MINCZESKI
The Spiders
The Reconstruction of Light
Gravity
Concert at Chopin's House: A Collection of Polish-American Writing

AKRON SERIES IN POETRY
Elton Glaser, Editor

Barry Seiler, *The Waters of Forgetting*
Raeburn Miller, *The Comma After Love: Selected Poems of Raeburn Miller*
William Greenway, *How the Dead Bury the Dead*
Jon Davis, *Scrimmage of Appetite*
Anita Feng, *Internal Strategies*
Susan Yuzna, *Her Slender Dress*
Raeburn Miller, *The Collected Poems of Raeburn Miller*
Clare Rossini, *Winter Morning with Crow*
Barry Seiler, *Black Leaf*
William Greenway, *Simmer Dim*
Jeanne E. Clark, *Ohio Blue Tips*
Beckian Fritz Goldberg, *Never Be the Horse*
Marlys West, *Notes for a Late-Blooming Martyr*
Dennis Hinrichsen, *Detail from* The Garden of Earthly Delights
Susan Yuzna, *Pale Bird, Spouting Fire*
John Minczeski, *Circle Routes*
Barry Seiler, *Frozen Falls*

John Minczeski

Circle Routes

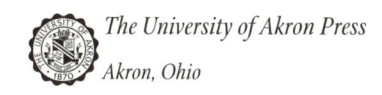

The University of Akron Press
Akron, Ohio

©2001 by John Minczeski
All rights reserved

Cover painting by Pupino Samonà.
Cover design by Kachergis Book Design.

I would like to thank the following journals which published versions of many of these poems:

Agni: "Trains That Run on Time"; *The Cape Rock:* "The Other"; *Crania:* "My Brother Flies Solo," "Great Circle Routes"; *Cream City Review:* "Note to Trish from the Flamingo Motel, Long Prairie, Minnesota"; *Free Lunch:* "Work"; *Great River Review:* "Sunday Morning at the Laundromat," "Monet Paints His Wife's Portrait on Her Death Bed," "Excelsior Amusement Park, 1932"; *Marlboro Review:* "Mayflies," "Sassafras," "Caterpillars at Knossos"; *Meridian:* "Pencil in the Concentration Camp"; *Mid-American Review:* "Bats," "Liberation"; *Midwest Quarterly:* "Bronislaw and the Devil"; *Pemmican:* section five of "Labyrinth"; *Pleiades:* "Iris."

I would also like to thank The Saint Paul Companies for a generous grant which gave me time to complete this manuscript, the Jerome Foundation for a travel grant, The Corporation of Yaddo, Toni Maraini for permission to quote a fragment of her poem, "Se Passa Afrodite" in "Pencil in the Concentration Camp," and to the following individuals who gave me much needed advice and encouragement: Alvaro Cardona-Hine, the remarkable community at The Warren Wilson Program for Writers, Janet Holmes, Terri Ford, Dan Tobin, Martha Rhodes, my teachers and mentors, my music collaborator Carei Thomas, Carolyn Holbrook for her continued faith in me, Jim Dochniac, my Dante group affectionately known as *l'Amici d'Inferno*, Carolyn Wright and Francine Sterle for the careful reading they gave to many of these poems in earlier drafts. My unending thanks and admiration go to Topazia Alliata, who inspired many of these poems. To my wife, Joan, none of this would have been possible without her.

All inquiries and permission requests should be addressed to the Publisher, The University of Akron Press, 374B Bierce Library, Akron, Ohio 44325-1703.

LIBRARY OF CONGRESS CATALOGING-IN-PUBLICATION DATA

Minczeski, John.
   Circle routes : poems / by John Minczeski.—1st ed.
     p. cm. — (Akron series in poetry)
   ISBN 1-884836-76-3 (alk. paper) — ISBN 1-884836-77-1 (pbk. : alk. paper)
   I. Title. II. Series.
PS3563.I4635 C57 2001
811'.54—DC21

                                            2001002655

Manufactured in the United States of America
The paper used in this publication meets the minimum requirements of American National Standard for Information Sciences—Permanence of Paper for Printed Library Materials, ANSI Z39.48-1984. ∞

First Edition

For Topazia Alliata

Contents

One

State of the Art   3
Bronislaw and the Devil   4
Afterwards   6
The Other   7
Iris   8
Great Circle Routes   10
Mayflies   12
My Brother Flies Solo   14
Excelsior Amusement Park, 1932   16
Ponte Garibaldi   17

Two

Trains That Run on Time   21
Paper   22
Pencil in the Concentration Camp   25
Liberation   26
Water   27
Stone Buddhas   29

Three

Gallery, *Via degli Angeli Scuri*   33
The Corporal   35
Waverly Place   37
Colosseum   39
Monet Paints His Wife's Portrait on Her Deathbed   40
A Bat   41
Louie, Louie   44
Caterpillars at Knossos   46
Work   48
Sunday Morning at the Laundromat   49
On Muffing a Translation Concerning Aphrodite   50
Labyrinth   52

Four

    Note to Trish from the Flamingo Motel,
        Long Prairie, Minnesota   59
    An Empty Glass   61
    Crows at Sunset   64
    Mosquitoes   66
    Webs   68
    Sassafras   70

ONE

State of the Art

On a jackhammer morning
that could be September, a crow banks
around the house next door, followed
by three pigeons a minute later. Do you
still think there are no random events in the universe,
Herr Heisenburg? Other birds—sparrows—
hop across my roof and peer over the edge.
Oh, the pure outrage of crows in the distance,
followed by restrained, Poe-like dignity

as a funnel of silence crosses the yard
disguised as a peregrine. A sparrow crouches
to become a knot on a dead branch; even
the wind stalls, silencing the chimes.
Two seconds, three at best, and a squirrel
clatters up the drain pipe; a siren with breath boxes

scrambles down Hamline Avenue.
Anything else in this synchronicity boat,
Dr. Jung? Roofers clawing
through old shingles? The phlox with blown beards
drooping like Spanish moss? Something
besides these crows
whose ink I dip my pen into,
shouting themselves hoarse?

Bronislaw and the Devil

What can he know, never straying
from the dirt floors of the farm,
each year a commissar gathering
the tsar's portion of wheat, pigs,
and sons who'd come of age?

Or that the first day in New York,
his elation would shrink to nothing
when he froze in the middle of a street,
teamsters shouting, *Get out of the road,
you goddam Polack*, gawking

at the first black man he'd ever seen?
Among delivery vans, ice wagons,
and vegetable vendors, how could he guess
Lucifer's too dazzling for naked eyes,
or that forty-five years from then

he'd be selling houses in South Bend
to black families moving in
as Polish families moved out?
Right now he's not thinking *Angel*
or *Black Madonna of Czestochowa*;

he's thinking the cold knuckle of hell,
he's fingering the worthless *zlotys* in his pocket
and the crumpled address
of someone from his village.
Citizens of the old world

look for relatives in the new;
a man he thinks is the devil
rounds a corner between the Battery
and Wall Street.
How can I not love him

standing there, surrounded
by chaos in the street,
as he tries to think if he can hide
or run back to the boat, or take one
step forward and start bargaining?

Afterwards

They told how my mother walked the floor
from midnight to dawn the day I was born,
my father pacing between flights on his D.C. run.

Afterwards, hazy from anesthesia,
she asked for me. They gave her a stuffed rabbit to hold,
a shot of phenobarbital for amnesia,

and bundled me to her the next day,
my nose no longer smushed like a flounder
from the birth canal. She took it on faith

I had not been replaced as I studied the world
—her face and hands, the bottle
they slipped between my gums—

with the seriousness of a Presbyterian minister.
Looking through the nursery window,
visiting hours over—a father's duty,
in those days, satisfied nine months before—

he said I looked like every other baby
in the ward: *crying for attention,*

*forlorn and wizened, and red-faced
as any old wino.*

The Other

You were the one who sweet-talked
good grades out of Sister Josephine,
while I sat in the back staring at snowflakes
big as galleons and shipwrecks.

In March, we were wings on the same biplane,
a snap roll just off the runway. In April,
we carried the torches and torpedoes of lilacs.

Remember being a cat rubbing darkness
under wildflowers all those lifetimes ago,
watching wind ruffle a jay's feathers?

First you were the snake
biting a woman's ankle by a creek,
then you became the woman herself
who almost made it back to the world,

but near the tunnel mouth, trying to gulp
the first strands of sweet air, you cried out
from the light, or the stab of air
that stuck in your throat
the instant you left the world. Now

when I look back down the stairs
I see at best a shadow curled in other shadows.
Usually it is a bat, that ultrasonic trick of night.
Other times it is nothing: some twig
falling through the streetlight's glare like ice.

Iris

The iris, those fleshpots,
are at it again—it must
be May—exploding
among the emerald bodies
of dragonflies, bobbing
in the slightest breeze,
thinking nothing—as in
Hold the night for me,
I feel faint; as in *Heartbreak,*
you got any other tunes
in there?

Nine-tenths water,
one-tenth purple soufflé,
and what starts life
as boxing gloves
ends with the smell
of bridesmaids.
Will they ever wear
these things again?
Will they be here tomorrow

after the hailstorm
and neighborhood children
pausing in hide and seek—
with no size limits
or catch and release?

With their furry black tongues
beside the circular staircases
of lilies, what will they whisper
when that wild purple
goes invisible at midnight?

Great Circle Routes

This window, clear waterfall,
keeps nothing of light that rests
on the tongues of plants, no photographs
of stars, nothing of a jet's dryness
clinging to great circle routes—

>but in 1929, at this very window
>you could hear Speed Holman's engine snarl
>as he flattened the propeller's pitch
>and throttled back on base leg
>to his home field by the fairgrounds.

The ghost in knickers and argyle socks
caught lying on our bed one night
could have heard the biplane, even seen it
looping the loop through the high bridge.
Damn, I can hear him saying, *hot damn!*

>On May 17, 1931, during his signature stunt,
>an outside loop, Holman's safety belt broke.
>How many times had he done this? Upside down,
>a hundred feet off the runway, held snug
>by the same belt, the same white corrosion
>eating the anchor bracket?

Time is like this. In my father's double exposures,
my uncles and aunt, stern and Polish,
stand next to the brick house on Brookfield;
superimposed on them, my mother—

months before I become a tiny secret
inside her—leans against a Globe Swift
at the Cleveland Air Races, smiling.

        It is these spring mornings
        where cows wander down
        to shadowy freedoms of pasture;
        it's the sound of bees mired
        in quadratic equations of lilacs,
        sucking light from the blossoms.

Mayflies

Two years underwater,
and now two days to finish
their mission on earth
before a swallow ends it for them
or a trout, before the sun
dries them out, before
their two days dry up.

Not of the order *True Flies,*
they squirm out of their old bodies,
the fragile seaweed of gills,
emerging into adulthood
with lungs and wings,
learning in ten seconds everything
they will ever know of flight.

And to avoid temptation
from the real job
—sex, sex, sex—
there's no mouth,
not even a straw
to sip the water they flutter on.

What was God thinking!
Can one appetite negate the other,
making desire so weak in one so small?

Two days, at most, of frenzy,
then spinning down
to lay their eggs, soundless as wind,

their new lungs unsuited
to the water that gave them birth,
their cellophane wings splayed
and useless as broken paddles.

My Brother Flies Solo

The sky's hard and splintery:
gray patches of snow, gray trees
scratching upward, the whole world
lacking color back then.

In the black and white snapshot,
a J-5 Cub is just lifting off
the frozen sod
of Chain O'Lakes Field.

At five hundred feet, it banks downwind
for another landing. Again and again.
My father steps into the flight shack
to warm himself with stale coffee,

his pride growing more routine
with each takeoff and landing.

> *In twenty years, drunk and desperate,*
> *his own son dying, my brother will call*
> *from California, wanting to steal a B-17*
> *to bomb the shit out of the Ayatollah.*
>
> *It will feel as though the war had never ended,*
> *and the gods still bargain*
> *over what they'll give up*
> *for the destruction of Troy:*
>
> *the waiting, the doctors' predictions, the chemo.*
> *Promising to take up flying again,*
> *everything, he tells his son, will be fine.*

As he brings the J-5 over the fence
at forty-five or fifty, as he touches down
and adds power to go around again,
he can see how brown the world is,

how blue with white patches of snow and ice.
But how small the plane looks from here.
If it weren't for the bad exposure,
this could be a Japanese painting: a few trees

lining the road north of the field,
the tiny airplane with my brother's face
behind shiny plexiglass,
and all this sky.

Excelsior Amusement Park, 1932

Captain Jack Payne, thick as a bulldog,
isn't smiling atop the hundred-foot ladder—
it's the Depression, after all. He licks
a finger to the wind and waits, ready
to lean forward, a jackknife
slicing through blazing water.

A loaf of bread only costs a nickel,
but the show's free, bless you, sirs.
Of course, the tank's deeper
than five feet—Captain Jack's no fool—
and he only climbs eighty rungs.
What the rubes don't know won't hurt.

The crowd presses against the ropes
to watch him fall according to the formula
Galileo calculated when everything
—souls and thought—was supposed to rise.
Captain Jack stands, shoulders squared,
on a swaying plank in the sky,

in the infinity of wind, solid American
syllables blaring from the loudspeaker:
Whenever you're ready, Captain!
Pressing against the ladder, he waits
for the final metallic words to reach him:
And good luck on your downward *journey.*

Ponte Garibaldi

That first year in Rome when the language
was stones under my tongue,
I stopped a businessman
by the post office to bum a cigarette

and ask where was *Putta Garibaldi*.
He looked at me with astonished eyes.
Yes, he had heard correctly:
a scruffy, twenty-year-old American, smoking

a pungent *Filtro,* calling Italy's great unifier
a whore. *Putta Garibaldi,* I said again,
do you know where? He had no words,
and raised his nose,

setting sail toward less turgid air.
I could wander hours
until I found a familiar landmark—
Via del Corso or the Pantheon—

or finish the cigarette and catch a bus,
for the morning air was full of cabbages
and carnations thrown in the street
after a grand party. Whose?

I asked no one else,
but they all knew; that much was clear.

Two

Trains That Run on Time

In the beginning, a few
said it didn't matter.

Among hells *they'd* choose the Italian one:
practiced inefficiency, great food,

green lizards hanging,
little minotaurs, on the walls.

The perfect rotors of maple seeds
lend the possibility of a forest,

and there is a certain elegance
in possibility, like a chess match.

It had been noticed
the company she kept:

Jewish artists and intellectuals.
Certain "friends" mentioned their concern

for her health. It was certain
she could be saved. It was spring,

almond trees blooming; the pines of Rome
still towered over eternity.

Paper

1
The table's set with steaming
pasta, but first the business
of his birthday—cuff links from his mother,

a handbound copy of his dissertation, *Secrets
of Tibet,* from his young wife,
his father's gift in a long box.

Wrapping paper flutters around his chair.

Here the joking stops
as he opens the lid and looks
into a concentration camp. No,

not that exactly, not yet, but close enough
as when lightning knocks you down
but doesn't kill. Tearing the ID papers,
the certificate of membership in half,

he flings them with the Fascist lapel pin
against the wall: *Non sono fascista,* he snaps,
turning and stalking like Orlando Furioso
out the door, slamming it behind.

2
Knowing he would never apply
for membership, his father took it on himself,
cashing favors with party faithful:

*to overlook reports you've been seen
with Jewish artists. You don't
have to wear a black shirt*

*or raise a stiff arm like a fucking erection
every time* il Duce's *name's mentioned,
but you could at least flash the party badge,*

*land a job here in Florence, something
in the department of antiquities. Who
do you think you are, tearing the family like this?*

3
The young wife watches him
storm out the other door, slamming it, too.
No third door to escape by,

should she pick at the abandoned food
or join her weeping mother-in-law
in the solidarity of hunger?

4
But there *was* a door, his professor told him,
for his degree in Asian Studies, and no requirement
of party membership—you don't need more

than an ounce of intelligence to decide—
Tokyo, teaching Dante with nothing,
outside of passports, bearing a Fascist signature.

5
Five years, maybe six, his wife
learning Japanese from her children,

the children's way of speaking—no blame,
the *I Ching* says—learning

the good manners to be comfortable
in another's company without speaking.

If only the starched officer standing at the door
observed the same custom.

Anti-fascists have taken over Italy.
You must pledge allegiance to Mussolini

or henceforth be an enemy of Japan.

6
They have learned to bow and show respect,
to smile politely at bad news: *Sorry, we know*

this must pain you, handing the loyalty pledge back,
immaculate and unsigned.

Pencil in the Concentration Camp

Scratched down to the nub,
some guard tossed it to the side
like a cigarette butt.

But there were more words left in it,
and more than cigarettes, pencils
you had to sharpen with your nails

were snatched up and hoarded,
hidden in straw mattresses
with scraps of paper.

She drew roosters
and pigs for her children,
red circles of an ibis's flight.

She gave them English
and the grave accents of Italian.
No paper too small,

she could hide her journal
in a shoe. Messages in a bottle?
No, these were mountains.

A haiku to hang
from the plum tree
and give to the wind,

her children watching

at the end of snaky cursive trails,
the pencil's tongue sniffing paper.

LIBERATION

After the surrender, the guards
piling into trucks and leaving the smell of dust behind,

before American soldiers came to liberate them,
allied planes parachuted C-rations, powdered milk,

canned peaches. How to be other than grateful?
No longer needing to snare birds

and snakes when the guards starved them,
they improvised a can opener

and rehydrated the powder
with the juice of peaches.

For two weeks, until transport arrived
and a more civilized state, victory

was the smell of lumpy, yellow milk
on their children's breath.

WATER

Those years in the camp,
her daughters never had
a proper bath. Now, liberated

in a Tokyo hotel, they drain the tub
and start again. *Hotter, mother,*

their skin wrinkled
and white as lychee nuts. They drain
and fill, again and again. They squeak

like ears of corn,
like shitake mushrooms. *Bring carrots,*

mother, and pineapple! Hurry!
Slice some apples, please!
Bring all the milk you have!

        Oh, my prunes and raisins,
        aren't you done cooking yet?

No, mother, not
until tomorrow
at least!

What else dissolves besides years of
concentration camp in cracks
of their skin?

Nothing. Just
the unbuttoned joy of water,

giggling even as their mother comes in
with armloads of towels.

>	Dear children,
>	do you think I
>	can ever get you dry?

Stone Buddhas

Everyone had a stone Buddha
or silk scroll passed down the family
so they could wade in the past
with no fear of drowning.

After the war, it was all they had:
no chickens or goats; husbands
were like mulberry leaves
bruised purple in the fading year.

An earthquake can swallow you whole
like a raisin, no matter who you are.
But who wouldn't, given a choice,
trade the past for a month of milk and rice?

The generals heard she knew something
of Japanese art, took her to a table
of Buddhas and carved jade: what dynasty?
What would they fetch

on the open market? Sometimes life
was a picnic basket, sometimes black rain.
It was the price she gave ivory and jade—
earrings for young American wives,

a samurai sword for the den
for dollars stamped with a red *J*.
She set aside pieces too valuable, too beautiful
for a single person to own.

What did the museums pay for them?
Did they make the sellers rich? Who knows anymore.

Milk flowed in Japan again, the polished jade and stone
floating between two worlds.

Three

GALLERY, *VIA DEGLI ANGELI SCURI*

She spotted me across the room,
never having seen me before,
though we'd spoken, once, on the phone.

Still wearing her fur coat
for the snow that would come later,
she hugged me around the neck,

kissing me on both cheeks.
Why me, I thought,
and not Ilych, the brilliant one?

The champagne was bitter,
the paintings worse—
green highway tape on green background—

on Street of the Dark Angels,
but let me see them again.
Let me see the rain again,

and the angels stepping into it
night after night, the glimmer
she must have seen

that drew her to me,
my clothes drying
in the heat of my fever

(I thought the CIA would never find me
if I kept moving like a shark
through the labyrinth of streets),

in the dark that drove the solstice down,
in the solemn night.

The Corporal

Were the camp guards like crows
demanding compliance with bayonets,
or would they become crows next lifetime
like these in St. Paul, ordering us out
for inspection at first light?

I saw them mob a peregrine once
across the freeway, a small rabbit in its claws.
Weighed down, it barely kept ahead
as they tried to pluck its flight feathers
as they do to each other,

like the time I stood naked with a cigarette
at the induction station for my physical.
A corporal leaning against a metal cabinet
with a cigarette of his own
ran to me, shouting to put it out.

I looked at him standing
in front of my nose and, taking
a last satisfying drag,
crushed it under my shoe.
Some men in that room

would perish in 'Nam. Not us.
A chartered Greyhound
delivered me to a county courthouse
ninety miles from Chicago;
he stayed on, processing inductees.

But did he shrink into exhaustion
with the rest of the country
when the news showed helicopters
plucking civilians from the embassy roof?
I see him, for some reason, weeping

in front of Monet's haystacks
at the Art Institute. Not remorse exactly,
and not because we lost the war,
but something like the future
grown suddenly vast as oceans

of August corn, a grain elevator
and feed store opposite the boarded-up
movie house in his hometown,
one road leading in
and two leading away.

Waverly Place

Walking with my daughter
past the brownstones,
I can't pick out the one I visited
when I was twenty and just back from exile,
can't remember which steps I climbed,
which door, an inner courtyard
I looked over for almost a week.

It was the year the draft board
wanted me for a monthly quota,
the year I went by another name.
The CIA could be anyone: the guy

who helped carry my luggage
or the one who sat beside me
on the DC-8 from Rome,
saying he dearly loved flying
as he gripped his armrests on takeoff.

The friend I stayed with agonized
over his master's thesis, still angry
the fifty dollars he sent to Italy
went for room and board, not
the appendectomy.

It was May; peonies lingered faintly
in the dusk. *Who the hell
are you?* my friend's roommate asked.
How could I say?
The turnbuckles of that evening

were bolted in spongy wood and concrete;
I barely knew myself.

I'll tell you the truth: barely older
than runaways selling grass in Washington Square,
I could be disappeared any minute, and wanted
a child to leave behind—someone else's voice,
if not my own—before I vanished.

I didn't think to say, *I yam what I yam*,
Popeye the Sailor's mantra. Instead
I turned and walked toward Avenue of the Americas
and my own confusion.

Even now it sounds theological
under this deepening lobelia
and false indigo sky, *I yam
what I yam*, walking with my daughter
toward the same Avenue of the Americas.

I visit so rarely. She leads
through the crowd
passing street vendors, fire hydrants,
window after storefront window,
turning frequently
as a mother might, careful

I don't get swallowed by a window display
or subway grate and fall behind
like a rowboat swept out in the tide,
the crowd filling the gap between us.

Colosseum

Stacked ten deep, German and Japanese tourists
peered down at the cells, the labyrinth
under the rotted-away floor, imagining lions
and Christians, gladiators and Christians,
imagining themselves as extras
in history's Cinemascope, martyrs
exiting straight to heaven,
the foppish emperor helping them
with a bored thumbs down.

Outside the walls, vendors sold
Ektachrome slides and postcards
and toy army guys who crawled on camouflaged elbows
and knees. Every few inches, they stopped
to fire their machine guns, *budabuda-
budabuda.* Almost as big as GI Joes,
they patrolled the Colosseum,
the tourists corralled inside,
the rest of us standing out here.

By the forum, university students disguised
as skeletons marched to drums and music.
She sipped peach nectar from a paper carton
for her sore throat. She should have been in bed,
but it was carnival. As they drew closer, we began
making out the words on their sagging banner:
Death to. . . . Then came the black standard
and insignia of the National Socialists.

Monet Paints His Wife's Portrait on Her Deathbed

There is so little money, he writes to a friend,
he can afford neither paint nor canvas—
yet here he is, layering white and blue,
a touch of red, the final colors at his disposal.

Where else put grief
if not these half-dozen strokes against a shawl?
His final gesture, blue-white like the others,
slashes across her still breast, the rose

near her heart. Her graying face, nearly lost
among pillows and bed linen, grows as indistinct
as his paintings of Vétheuil reflected in foggy water.
But there is no reflection here—nothing

that remains steady in the agitated current
other than her body, light
striking her pillow like a wedding veil.

A Bat

1
Taking down the curtains, she found a patch
of shadow-brown
grappled in cracked plaster
like a stranded mountaineer.

Clamping its tiny mouth with a towel,
I carried it to the upstairs porch. Instead
of a flutter of moleskin to the honeysuckle,

it dropped like an anchor
to the evening primrose,
that thatch of full moons by the cellar door.
What is it frowns on daytime flight?

Should I have carried it down
and pressed it into the box elder's striated bark?
And how could I tell if it was a little brown bat
or endangered Eastern Pipistrelle?

The cat, already outside,
felt the faint thud of manna.
He slinked forward, he
of the lion's clan, under

the leaves of phlox and cardinal flowers.

2
August. Searching
for a spot to hibernate,
one slips into the house
like a drunk

at closing time, invisible
but for the tachycardia
of its wings, and I
remember again

how well the world gets along
without me:
the double-flowering plum
doubling its annual quota

of leaves, the linked-arm solidarity of elms
broken by a single beetle.
When I net it
and carry it to the porch

to let it go,
another bat flashes outside
against the light. The heart
in anguish can do no less.

The year my daughter
closed down the muffin shop
weeknights at the mall,

I'd have to wait until I heard
her car in the driveway, her key
in the front door

before I could sleep.
One wing dangles
through the strings of the net

like a ragged flag.
It hisses
like a cardboard box
dragged across the floor.

By dawn, I've been up hours,
sleep broken by adrenaline
and the thought
another broken heart

could squeeze through a crack
the size of a dime
for the sugar of warmth,
some dry and dark

promised land
for the next six months,
like an aircraft hangar
or my attic; and how many

must be here already,
sleeping until the miracles
of March unfold: insects
and the enveloping skin of night.

Louie, Louie

It didn't matter what the words meant;
we sang along anyway, cranking the car radio
until the Delco speaker fuzzed out,
windows rolled down past Van Buren's on Portage,
Louie, Lou-eye,

the name we'd given him
in ninth grade, and it was almost enough
to make him fit in.
On his black corduroy jacket, *Louie,*
as though someone had scribbled across his heart

with orange thread. A sneer like Elvis's, a gift
to see the world rusting at its weld joints.
A friend's Studebaker Lark, even after
the valve job and new rings, would remain
an oil-burning pile of shit. *Assholes,*

he said at lunch, looking at the sports heroes,
the National Honor Society;
assholes, the perky cheerleaders
sitting among them; *assholes,*
from the back of World History.

Oh for a can of spray paint:
assholes on the beige tile of the gym walls.
No one saw him turn his back on us
that last time—jacket embroidered with four aces
and the king of hearts, a Roman short sword
stuck in its head.

Biking to pick up papers for my route,
I passed him just over the Michigan Street Bridge.
Textbooks and loose-leaf papers
floated down the St. Joseph River,
joining sewage and industrial run off

and Louie was smiling—
for once in his life carrying nothing
but sweet air. "You've been in airplanes,"
he said, "you must know how it feels."

I said I did, but how could I?
The weightlessness and gravity
of a happiness that absolved him
from having to suffer school
and its hierarchies, the daily insomnia

of teachers, the creeping stoicism of detention.
Just before I pedaled ahead, needing
to deliver the evening edition,
he looked from the afternoon traffic
on Michigan Street to the rose garden in Leeper Park

and, raising his arm like a sixteen-year-old pontiff,
blessed the world and everything in it,
where for the first time
it was all turning up aces.

Caterpillars at Knossos

The line of caterpillars, red and black,
yellow and black, undulated like a snake
along the wooden railing by the courtyard
and, without looking, I put my hand down

and felt their furry tube, as thin as the snake
Cleopatra tucked between her breasts,
or the one that bit Linda on the ankle
in Italy. But Linda at least has a knack

for surviving: the snake wasn't poisonous;
we didn't have to sing her back from Hades.
Last winter, after a guy ran a red light
and smacked her through an intersection,

she was on crutches until June.
I'm not sure about these caterpillars—
after I touch them, they break
some neural connection and lie

sprawled every which way
like cars in a train wreck, each
trying to find the ass of the one ahead.
Still, they've survived wind and earthquake,

four thousand years of Minoans and tourists,
line after conga line of caterpillars, up and down
the stone steps of Knossos, through light wells
and courtyards, into the hall of the double axe.

What secrets do they trade while joined?
They're like teenagers signing yearbooks,
telling each other never to change
just before they all change,

looking for a quiet spot
to spin their mummy cases.
When we next see them, Daedalus
should look so good, and Icarus,

as he throws himself toward the sun,
already knows he'll escape this labyrinth

the old-fashioned way and not by air,
as sweet as that is, and not by bus, as we do.

Work

All week it has rained,
pumping out green
and red-yellow buds on roadsides.

Today the tenth graders stare
at the walls in homeroom,
avoiding windows where they can see,

across the blacktop, a field
cobbled with frost-heaved rock.
After school, some will pick

the one sure crop farmers dread,
working for car payments
and gas money, and tomorrow will sit

waiting for someone to buzz them
from one classroom to another.
At least the walls are constant,

unlike these trees where next week
the green mist will coagulate like smoke
into leaves. At tilling time and harvest,

they'll steer around the piled rocks
and remember lifting and grunting,
the daily sweat,

the daily blank spaces of these walls
where they can barely wait
to start the real work of this world.

Sunday Morning at the Laundromat

As the grilles of pickups
nose over the sidewalk
like jet fighters ready to scramble,

anxious dogs in the front seats
watch their owners
sitting before the lenses

of front-loading Speed Queens.
As others dress for sermons,
a Dixie cup of powdered detergent

goes for thirty-five cents here. A man enters,
nodding to the others who barely glance up;
he respectfully lifts another man's coffee

for the *Sports Illustrated* beneath.
No talk shows on TV, no pregame.
The machines cycle through wash

and rinse, penance and absolution,
the men waiting until the dryers stop,
then folding socks and T-shirts

with a tenderness once reserved
for girlfriends and ex-wives.

On Muffing a Translation
Concerning Aphrodite

for Toni Maraini

Yes, it *was* Aphrodite, with her goddess eyes
and moist lips, listening to me
give her permission (permission!)
to go looking for eternity,

the one thing, along with beauty, she has
the most of. As for beauty, that truth serum,
any hand mirror will suffice. Lucky, mirrors
didn't shatter when I looked into them,

or some god grab me by the scruff
and drag me clear to the other side. Lucky,
anything that could be used against me,
an old running shoe or withered apple,

wasn't. As for ruining the conjugation
that made Aphrodite decipher those papyrus scrolls,
Aphrodite rub myth from dusty rocks,
I can only say Rome was dazzling:

carnival revelers roamed the streets until dawn—
trumpets and guitars, the bees
in the Barberini Palace still buzzing
these five hundred years. Watching

them from my window,
how could I notice *her*

sitting on the bed, waiting,
with the cool breeze of her gaze,

to set the words spinning
like a halo around my head?
Impatient, I licked and sealed the envelope
and fed the poem to a letter box

before I could think better of it,
as is often the case: neither truth *nor* beauty
but a freight train shuttling between,
the tracks still being laid.

Labyrinth

Stop me if you've heard this:
a young man calls home,
slurring like a lovesick ape: come bail him
out of jail. It's 3 A.M. and his father, blood
pounding at his temples but relieved
knowing at least *where* his son is, says

Stay right there. It might do you some good.

൹

It's nothing new. King Minos
hired the best architect to build his kid a jail
with the twisting, dark alleys he loved.
Day and night, workers fit stone against stone
with the precision of Mayas and caddis nymphs,

like workers preparing the port village
for tourist season: grouting and polishing tile,
stocking the Musicbar downstairs
with alcohol, power tools sounding like mosquitoes
through the night. And in the winding alleys,
a man pulls a fish in his wagon
past shop windows full of our daily bread.

The king's son—scraggly beard, head
like two bowling balls fused together—
roams faithfully inside the borders
until he lurches finally
like a Slinky having done its trick
of walking downstairs.
For all things tend toward entropy,

except the city kept growing, the jail
becoming what we all have:
in time, horses and taxis; in time, motorbikes
and jet fighters scrambling two by two
from the air base across the mountains;

dancing girls, a wild animal show.
A city like any other—you stop for coffee,
gulls make minor adjustments as they scour
the harbor for herring and anchovy.

As for the other kid, pick your own thread:
he finds a way of loosening time, letting it slip
through his fingers like a belt until he's released
the next day or the day after, wearing
the unreadable eyes of his old man.

૭

I dreamed we were shooting baskets—
the sound of ball on rim, the rim snapping back,
slap of feet on pavement. I missed a pass
and chased it into an opening in the brick,
you following to pass the ball in.

Inside, a dull light glowed
like a subway tunnel, the rose-colored walls
streaked with darker red. Behind us, solid stone
and rock like the wall of a church;
before us, no basketball.

Just as we were ready to split up
and meet back here, another player stuck his arm in
and dragged us out
through unbroken rock.

༄

There are times you see someone stumbling
in the deep pocket of morning after the music
grinds down, blinking hard against the light,
bumping against a wall
as though looking for another way in,

༄

the way the grizzly at Como Zoo swings his head
against the stone wall
until the top of his skull gleams white as bone; he rocks

his right foot behind him, balancing the motion of his head,
smoothing the top of his piled turds swarming with flies,
working his way into rock, the only way out.

༄

You might have heard the guards stood by
as other inmates looped a belt around his neck,
hoisting him on the bars like a suicide. *Fucking rich kid,
stay where you belong.*

Like gulls heading inland
to pick over the market stalls at dusk,
I imagine the boy soaring over his house,
calling in some bird language.

His father, going to the balcony, hears the whine
of scooters in front of the harbor restaurants,
the patrons' loud voices in the dark below.

Chania, Crete

Four

Note to Trish from the Flamingo Motel, Long Prairie, Minnesota

for Patricia Hampl

Last time I was here the *Challenger* exploded
across America—the boosters' white plumes
twisting until it looked oddly beautiful
against the sky's dark blue. Now,
the week after Thanksgiving, Christmas lights

blossom on trees, outline entire houses
in flashing color. The guy who had a coronary last week
is bolting a sleigh to his roof. On Tuesday, my guide
pointed out the toy collector's house, a maroon
and cream Schwinn in his picture window,
as though Christmas had arrived early;
the corner where all summer a man waves
at passing cars; the house of the child molester
who had to leave his clothes behind

when they hauled him to jail. High school kids
drive back from the dance hall in Browerville
through the roll call of alcohol. Some work
graveyard shift at the packing plant and sleep
through morning classes. Long Prairie, Minnesota.
From the hills, it looks like a postage stamp,
and I could see myself here, so help me,

greasing my skin to keep from cracking,
loading logs into the fire nights like this,
and hunkering down like the cold itself
released at last from the driving wind.

An Empty Glass

1
At dinner, he toasted us
with an empty glass,
my fellow expatriate,
as though it could explain

the sound of one hand,
the state of enlightenment
that links nothing and everything
by a logical thread
like a tin-can telephone.

2
Later that night, he watched cities
boil down to clouds of lava,
earth itself evaporating to cosmic plankton.

While January rain
cooled paving stones
in the piazza outside,
everything here was Hindenberg

and Blake's visions: stars going nova,
whole galaxies collapsing into teacups
and thimbles, into the single, round eye
of a hummingbird.

3
We've all lived
slightly in the future,
but he grabbed the chance,
before oceans turned to gasoline,

to glimpse his own:
scorn and sackcloth,
FBI agents meeting his plane
at Kennedy International,

the eventual flight to Halifax.
Even you, he said, seeing me

write this thirty years later,
will betray me. And then
the end came

4
and kept coming. Close-ups
of Rome and Hong Kong imploding
like newsreels of atomic tests,

and I couldn't tell if his tears
were for the end of humanity
or his own misunderstood self.

5
I am standing up
and going to bed
as I always do in this moment,

so I don't know what happens next:
if he says the spirit is willing

but the flesh is weak, if he
forgives us, Father,
we know not what we do.

Crows at Sunset

for John Engman

He had lain on the floor most of the night,
and in the morning, when they found him,
two days in a hospital bed,

with none of that wry humor,
the smell of cigarettes and stale beer
on student papers he handed back.

In the funeral home, holding his mother's
soft hand, I didn't say how he reminded me
of Cavafy: secretary by day, poet by night,

or the irony his full medical coverage
—finally, after all these years—
couldn't help in the end. The evening he died,

a flock of crows, hundreds, rose with a single cry
at the end of my street, blocking out
the sun. I don't like putting *evening*

in a poem about a friend's death,
but the crows suddenly veered toward me
like someone flipping Venetian blinds,

the brilliant sun flashing orange through them,
and they disappeared, leaving only that cry
magnified by a hundred voices

until they wheeled north
toward winter again, absorbing the sun
in their glossy wings, suddenly more solid

than the blacktop they rose from.

Mosquitoes

Were angels ever so happy?
Or nurses, hypo in hand, repeating their mantra?

A drop of Novocain,
a hint of anticoagulant, and

as a resort owner once told me,
let enough of them bite,

you'll never have a coronary.
So all is Zen mind among the swarm,

and the little pimple merely a postscript
to the love letter they leave behind.

So when July melts into August,
all is long sleeves and boots,

a smear of DEET and the lingering
aroma of a cheap cigar.

Though corpses of fallen comrades
surround my green chair,

they can't resist the dark lure
under my skin, and fresh squadrons

pick up my scent. I can hear
the drone of their multiple engines

like the Flying Tigers. Behind
those grinning sharks' teeth,

another John Wayne's adjusting his goggles,
radioing his wing man:

Cover me, Blackie.
I'm going in.

Webs

Slipping down to tuck in
her latest visitor,
she sees it's a yellow-jacket
and scurries back to safety

in the corner of her web.
For this is no mosquito
with a life instinct as short
as a toothpick in a vice-grip;

this wasp is tearing the house apart,
swinging like a clapper
in a broken bell

until it tears free
and flies straight to its nest
in the ground,
its hoard of venom, an idle harem.

The next day, webs as complex
as Gaudi's apartment building
cover my lawn furniture;

a tightrope walker's net
holds a wooden kitchen match
with the sunlit texture of morning,

and late summer has a just-made look
like whitewashed buildings

lining the harbor
before tourists settle in:

a little message letting you know
how important you are,
that we need you
more than you need us, dear traveler.

Sassafras

Say it's spring. The sassafras's top branches
curve up like the horns of Isis
on this wind-strummed island—
body of lyre, secret tuning fork
propping up the sky so long
night must come in a brilliant flash
on pine needles. Say Clifford Brown's

alive in the house, talking to a piano
and bass like the lighthouse at West Chop.
Here, in this deepening blue sky,
these unbleached clouds, is the hawk
I earlier mistook for a crow.
Say it's May. Say I love you.

About the Author

John Minczeski, a native of South Bend, Indiana, lives in St. Paul, Minnesota, teaching poetry in elementary schools and colleges throughout the state. He has an MFA in creative writing from the Warren Wilson Program for Writers. Winner of National Endowment for the Arts and Bush Foundation Artist fellowships, Minczeski has published three previous books of poetry, most recently *Gravity* (Texas Tech University Press, 1991).

About the Book

Circle Routes was designed and typeset by Amy Petersen. The typeface, StonePrint, was designed by Sumner Stone in 1991.

Circle Routes was printed on 60-pound Writers Natural and bound by Cushing-Malloy, Inc. of Ann Arbor, Michigan.

NORMANDALE COMMUNITY COLLEGE
LIBRARY
9700 FRANCE AVENUE SOUTH
BLOOMINGTON, MN 55431-4399